# How to *Write*
# 4 Types of Essays

Michael A. Putlack

DARAKWON

# How to *Write* 4 Types of Essays

**Author**  Michael A. Putlack
**Publisher**  Chung Kyudo
**Editors**  Kwak Bitna, Cho Sangik
**Designers**  Jang Meeyeon, Yoon Hyunju

First Published May 2019
By Darakwon Inc.
Darakwon Bldg., 211, Munbal-ro, Paju-si, Gyeonggi-do 10881
Republic of Korea

Tel. 82-2-736-2031 (Ext. 550)

Price ₩14,000
ISBN 978-89-277-0973-2  13740
http://www.darakwon.co.kr

Main Book

8 7 6 5 4 3 2     22 23 24 25 26

# Introduction

Writing is rapidly becoming a lost art. This is especially true in the Internet Age. These days, when many people write, they merely compose short text messages, emails, or social media posts, and they often litter their writing with emojis and emoticons rather than expressing their thoughts, feelings, opinions, and desires in complete sentences.

While people are not writing as much as they once did, being able to write well remains a valuable skill. This is especially true of writing essays. People who can write essays are capable of putting their thoughts into organized forms. Those individuals are also capable of creating arguments that can convince others of their points of view. They are additionally capable of using critical thinking skills to express their thoughts in written form.

Having writing skills is something employers highly value in their employees. Those individuals with good writing skills can effectively state their thoughts and make good arguments. Skills like those are of great importance in the workplace.

*How to Write 4 Types of Essays* was written with the objective of helping people learn the disappearing art of writing. Readers who use this book will learn about four different types of essays and how to write them. They will learn how to organize their essays properly, how to transfer their thoughts from their brains to paper, and how to make their writing effective at convincing the people reading it of whatever they are arguing. The book also provides readers with various tips on how to improve their writing skills.

Those individuals who utilize *How to Write 4 Types of Essays* will see the quality of their writing improve, and their thought processes will get better as well by virtue of their improved essay-writing skills.

I wish you the best of luck as you strive to improve your writing skills, and I hope you benefit greatly from using *How to Write 4 Types of Essays*.

*Michael A. Putlack*

# Scope and Sequence

| Chapter | Unit | | Reading | Writing Tips | Grammar |
|---|---|---|---|---|---|
| **1** **Expository Writing** p.9 | 1 | My Neighborhood in Thirty Years | Smart Homes: Houses of the Future | The Five-Paragraph Essay | will + verb, be going to + verb |
| | 2 | How to Improve Your Health | All Kinds of Exercise | Thesis and Topic Statements | have to + verb, must + verb, should + verb, ought to + verb |
| | 3 | How to Be a Good Friend | Positive Characteristics: Survey Results | Writing an Introduction | when |
| | 4 | The Water Cycle | Water Erosion | Writing a Conclusion | a, an, the |
| | 5 | How to Make Your Favorite Food | Dry-Heat and Moist-Heat Cooking | Sequence Words | and |
| **2** **Descriptive Writing** p.41 | 6 | Your Favorite Painting | New Art Gallery to Open | Formal and Informal Writing | because, because of |
| | 7 | The Rooms in Your Home | Hampton Realty | Transition Words | there is, there are |
| | 8 | Your Characteristics | The Introvert/Extrovert Quiz | Using Personal Examples | and, but, or, so |
| | 9 | A Place You Would Like to Visit | Travel Diary | Avoiding Unnecessary Adverbs | would + verb, would not + verb |
| | 10 | Your Favorite Class | Teaching Methods | Varying Sentence Length | adverbs of frequency |

| Chapter | | Unit | Reading | Writing Tips | Grammar |
|---|---|---|---|---|---|
| **3**<br>**Persuasive Writing**<br>p.73 | 11 | Recycling | Renewable and Nonrenewable Resources | Stating Opinions | gerunds |
| | 12 | Voting | Vote… Or Else! | Statistics | subjunctive mood |
| | 13 | Pets | Big Sale at Petland | Comparing and Contrasting | relative pronoun |
| | 14 | Chores | Chore Diary | Hyperbole | make, have |
| | 15 | Video Games | A Short Timeline of Video Games | Flow | by + gerund |
| **4**<br>**Narrative Writing**<br>p.105 | 16 | A Story from Your Country's History | Various Countries' Mythologies | Appositives | passive voice |
| | 17 | A Scary Moment in Your Life | Horror Film Week | Quotations | imperatives |
| | 18 | A Time When You Helped Someone | Volunteering | Familiar and Unfamiliar Words | infinitive |
| | 19 | The Last Trip You Took | Book the Trip of a Lifetime | Types of Sentences | compound predicate |
| | 20 | A Time You Learned a Valuable Lesson | Comments on a Blog | Avoiding Repetition | rather than + verb, rather than + verb -ing |

# How to Use This Book

There are many types of essays people can write. However, the four most common are expository, descriptive, persuasive, and narrative essays. These four types of essays are covered in detail in this book. Readers can feel free to read the book from beginning to end to learn about all four types of essays. They can also feel free to focus only on a specific chapter in order to improve their skills at writing a certain type of essay.

### Step 1   Answer Questions for Writing Assignment

This part contains the question that will be the focus of the unit. Readers can think about the question and consider how they are going to answer it.

### Step 2   Build Background

This part contains a reading passage of some type that is related to the topic of the unit. Readers can learn new words and expressions from the passage, and they can also start thinking about the question in more detail.

### Step 3   Brainstorm

*Building Ideas*

Readers can brainstorm on the topic by filling in the boxes with various ideas. The ideas readers come up with here can be used for the body paragraphs in their essays.

*Building Vocabulary*

This part contains vocabulary words related to the topic as well as their definitions. There are also some comprehension questions that test readers' understanding of the words and definitions.

### Step 4   Make an Outline

This part lets readers make an outline for their essay based on what they wrote down in the boxes for building ideas on the previous page.

### Step 5   Write a First Draft

In this part, readers write the first draft of their essay by using the outline they completed in the previous section.

## Step 6 · Learn a Writing Tip

This part contains a short essay about a skill that will make readers' writing ability better.

## Step 7 · Read a Model Essay

This part has a sample essay based on the question asked at the start of the unit (Writing Assignment). In each essay, the skill taught in the How to Make Your Writing Better section is emphasized, and readers are given the opportunity to learn how the skill can be used in the essay.

## Step 8 · Learn Grammar

This part contains a short grammar section focusing on an aspect of grammar found in the model essay. Readers can study the description of the grammar and look at the example sentences. Then, there is a section for writing sentences based on the grammar in this section.

## Step 9 · Self-Evaluate

This part contains twelve questions for readers to conduct a self-evaluation of the first draft of their essay.

## Step 10 · Write a Final Draft

This part lets readers revise their first draft and then write a final draft of their essay.

## Step 11 · Evaluate Your Partner's Essay

This part allows readers to find a partner, read their partner's essay, and then evaluate the positive and negative aspects of the essay to provide feedback for their partner by using the questions from the self-evaluation section on the previous page.

## Step 12 · Choose the Best Essay

In this part, readers should get into groups, read all of the essays, and then determine which individual wrote the best essay.

## Step 13 · Write about More Topics

This part contains five questions related to the topic of the unit. Readers can use these questions to write additional essays.

# 1

# Expository Writing

The purpose of **expository writing** is to explain, describe, or inform readers about a particular topic. Expository writing should focus on facts, and the writing should be logical and presented in a straightforward manner. This type of writing is often found in newspapers, magazines, journals, and encyclopedias. Many academic articles are also expository works.

In general, a work of expository writing can be divided into three parts: the introduction, the body, and the conclusion. The introduction is a single paragraph describing what the essay is about. The body contains several points—usually three—that prove or explain the information described in the introduction. The conclusion then sums up the information provided in the essay.

Here are some examples of expository writing.

**Example 1**
Hydroelectric power is obtained by using the power of running water to create electricity. This is accomplished by putting dams across rivers and by using flowing water to power turbines, which then make electricity. Hydroelectric power is typically cheap and is also a renewable source of energy. However, there are only a limited number of places where dams can be built on rivers. The reason is that dams create lakes behind them, which can affect local ecosystems. In addition, dams create problems for river traffic such as ships and barges.

**Example 2**
Vaccines are used to provide immunity to certain diseases for people. Most vaccines contain dead or weakened versions of a virus. They are then given to people by giving them a shot or by having them take the vaccine orally. The body's immune system recognizes the virus and creates antibodies to fight it. Later, if the actual virus is introduced to a person, then the antibodies immediately begin to destroy it. This keeps the person from becoming sick. In general, most vaccines provide many years of immunity to certain diseases.

# 01 My Neighborhood in Thirty Years

**WRITING ASSIGNMENT**  Think about what your neighborhood will be like in thirty years. How will it change? What will be better and worse?

**Building Background**  Read the following newspaper article. Then, answer the questions.

## Smart Homes: Houses of the Future

*by Peter Collins*

In the future, the homes people live in will change greatly. They will not look any different. But they will become much more convenient and efficient. These homes will be called smart homes.

Smart homes will become possible thanks to the Internet of Things. This is an integrated network that allows all kinds of electronic devices to be connected to the World Wide Web. This includes computers, TVs, air conditioners, and refrigerators. Someday soon, homeowners will not have to go shopping at supermarkets. Instead, their refrigerators will recognize when they are running low on milk, eggs, and other items. Then, they will order the items their residents need and have them delivered straight to the people's homes.

Smart homes will use this kind of technology in many ways. They will have smart devices connected to the Internet of Things. Smart homes will also have special sensors in the rooms. For example, when a person enters a room, the lights will turn on automatically, and the air conditioner will cool the room to the temperature that individual likes. The person's favorite music will start playing as well. When the person leaves the room, the light and air conditioner will turn off while the music will stop. In addition, if a thief tries to break in, the house will contact the police immediately.

These are just a few of the ways that smart homes will improve people's lives. As technology improves, people's quality of life in their homes will improve as well.

1  How will the Internet of Things change life in the future?

2  What do you think about smart homes? Would you like to live in one? Why or why not?

Think about the topic and brainstorm some ideas for your essay. Refer to the words and definitions below for help. Then, answer the questions.

## Building Ideas

### What Will My Neighborhood Look Like in 30 Years?

| Change 1 | Change 2 | Change 3 |
| --- | --- | --- |
|  |  |  |

## Building Vocabulary

**urban** *(adj)* related to a city

**suburban** *(adj)* related to a suburb

**rural** *(adj)* related to the countryside

**innovation** *(n)* a new idea or invention, often one that is a dramatic change or improvement

**energy efficient** *(adj)* using as little energy as possible

**sustainable** *(adj)* able to be supported or continued

**renewable** *(adj)* able to be used again

**recycle** *(v)* to treat items made of glass, metal, plastic, or paper in order to use them again

**solar power** *(n)* energy that is created from the sun's rays

**solar panel** *(n)* a piece of equipment that captures the sun's rays and turns them into energy

**nuclear energy** *(n)* electricity created from the splitting of the atom

**hydropower** *(n)* water energy; electricity created from flowing water, often by using a dam

**carpool** *(v)* to ride to work or school with one's coworkers or fellow students to save gas

**monorail** *(n)* an aboveground train whose cars drive on one track

**subway** *(n)* an underground train

**hyperloop** *(n)* an underground tube that uses a vacuum to transport people and goods quickly

**commuter train** *(n)* a train that runs from the suburbs to a downtown area

**electric car** *(n)* a car that uses electric batteries rather than gasoline to run

**self-driving vehicle** *(n)* a car that can drive itself and needs no human driver

**moving sidewalk** *(n)* a walkway that moves so that people do not have to walk themselves

**smart home** *(n)* a home with appliances and electronics connected to the Internet of Things

**skyscraper** *(n)* a very tall building

**green space** *(n)* an area with lots of plants such as a park or garden

**vertical farm** *(n)* an indoor farm that uses stacks of trays of crops to farm efficiently

*Fill in the blanks with the words above.*

1 Some cities plan to build _____ above the streets to move large numbers of people.

2 Many skyscrapers will contain _____ to provide food for their residents.

*Choose the correct words for the sentences.*

3 (Suburban / Rural) places are located right beside large urban areas.

4 Many company workers prefer to (recycle / carpool) to their offices with their colleagues.

## Making an Outline

Look at the ideas you came up with in the brainstorming section. Then, use them to create an outline for your essay.

### Introduction

### Body

| Detail 1 | Detail 2 | Detail 3 |

### Conclusion

## First Draft

Use the outline you wrote above to write the first draft of your essay.

# The Five-Paragraph Essay

The five-paragraph essay is one way to write a short essay. In this method, an essay has five paragraphs: an introduction, three body paragraphs, and a conclusion.

The introduction should describe the topic of the essay. It should also contain a thesis statement. This is one sentence that explains what the essay is about. The last sentence should contain a transition to the first body paragraph.

Each body paragraph should focus on a different point or argument. You should include the strongest point or argument in the first paragraph. Be sure to include examples in the body paragraphs to make your essay stronger. One sentence should also describe the content of the paragraph.

The conclusion should summarize the essay. It should have a concluding statement, which restates the thesis statement. It should then either explain a result of the body paragraphs or simply mention the arguments made in the body paragraphs.

**Model Essay**  Read the following sample essay. Underline the thesis statement and the concluding statement.

## My Neighborhood Thirty Years from Now

I live downtown in a large urban center. Thirty years from now, my neighborhood will look much different from today. The three main differences will be the sizes of the buildings, the types of transportation people use, and the way the Internet of Things will affect my neighborhood.

First, the buildings will be larger than today. Right now, my neighborhood has some large buildings. But there will be many buildings more than 100 stories high three decades from now. Building methods will improve, making it easier and faster to construct large buildings. People will live, work, and shop in these buildings.

Second, the methods of transportation used in my neighborhood are going to change. Most people in my neighborhood drive cars or ride on buses. In the future, fewer cars are going to be on the road. Instead, people are going to use buses and ride in monorails above the roads. For pedestrians, moving sidewalks are going to transport them from one place to another quickly.

Third, the Internet of Things will greatly improve my neighborhood. When a person is walking alone at night, streetlights will turn on to guide that person home safely. Buses will appear at bus stops when enough people are waiting for them. And when trashcans are full, the government will be alerted automatically. Then, garbage trucks will arrive to keep the neighborhood clean.

These are just a few of the changes that will happen in my neighborhood in thirty years. These changes will make my neighborhood a much better place to live. So more people will want to live there.

When talking about the future, you need to use the future tense. Use **"will + verb"** to make the future simple tense. You can use "will + verb" when making predictions about the future. You can also use **"be going to + verb"** to make future predictions.

- Building methods will improve. → Building methods are going to improve.

- Streetlights will turn on. → Streetlights are going to turn on.

- More people will want to live there. → More people are going to want to live there.

*Write two sentences with "will + verb" and two sentences with "be going to + verb."*

1 ........................................................................................................................

2 ........................................................................................................................

3 ........................................................................................................................

4 ........................................................................................................................

*Circle "will + verb" and "be going to + verb" in the essay on the previous page.*

## Self-Evaluation   Reread your first draft. Then, complete the following self-evaluation.

| | | | |
|---|---|---|---|
| 1 | Did I write a five-paragraph essay? | ☐ YES | ☐ NO |
| 2 | Did I include a thesis statement in the introduction? | ☐ YES | ☐ NO |
| 3 | Did I use examples in each body paragraph? | ☐ YES | ☐ NO |
| 4 | Did I include a topic statement in each body paragraph? | ☐ YES | ☐ NO |
| 5 | Did I restate the thesis statement in the conclusion? | ☐ YES | ☐ NO |
| 6 | Did I use correct grammar? | ☐ YES | ☐ NO |
| 7 | Did I use correct spelling? | ☐ YES | ☐ NO |
| 8 | Did I use correct punctuation? | ☐ YES | ☐ NO |
| 9 | Did I use sequence words properly? | ☐ YES | ☐ NO |
| 10 | Did I use transition words well? | ☐ YES | ☐ NO |
| 11 | Did I avoid using contractions? | ☐ YES | ☐ NO |
| 12 | Did I make logical arguments? | ☐ YES | ☐ NO |

**Final Draft**  Now, using the self-evaluation, write your final draft.

_____

_____

_____

_____

_____

_____

_____

_____

_____

_____

_____

_____

**Evaluate Your Partner's Essay**  Read your partner's essay and make positive and negative comments on it. Use the self-evaluation form on the previous page if you need help.

**Choose the Best Essay**  Divide into groups of four and read all of the essays. Then, decide which essay is the best. Discuss why you feel that way with your group members.

Look at the following topics. Choose one of them and write an expository essay.

**More Topics**

- What types of energy sources will people use twenty years from now?

- What will some popular jobs be in the next fifty years?

- How will the Internet of Things change people's lives in the future?

- What will it be like to live in a smart home?

- How will overpopulation affect the Earth in the twenty-first century?

# 02 How to Improve Your Health

**WRITING ASSIGNMENT**
Think about your health at the present time. How can you improve it? What actions and activities can you do to become healthier?

**Building Background** Read the following website article. Then, answer the questions.

https://www.exercisetoday.com/allkindsofexercise

## All Kinds of Exercise

**Writer** *Margaret Wilson*

Are you thinking of exercising but do not know what exactly you should do? You should consider why you want to exercise first. People often exercise to do cardio training, to increase the sizes of their muscles, and to improve their flexibility.

People doing cardio training want to strengthen their cardiovascular system, which is the heart and the lungs. There are numerous types of exercises to do this. Among them are walking, swimming, and dancing. Doing aerobics is also good for the cardiovascular system. There are many benefits to cardio training. It can reduce a person's body fat, strengthen the heart, and lower blood pressure. Cardio activities are often fun and easy to do as well.

When people want to strengthen their muscles, they normally lift weights. This is also known as resistance training. Lifting weights can increase people's strength, tone their bodies, and reduce problems such as lower back pain. In addition to lifting weights, people can do pushups and pullups and go mountain climbing to do resistance training.

The third main type of exercise is flexibility training. It can make people more limber, improve their balance and posture, and help them become more coordinated. There are several ways to improve one's flexibility, including yoga and Pilates.

So before you get started exercising, think about what exactly you want to work on. You do not have to choose a single type of exercise either. Try two or even three types of exercise, and you will not only have fun, but you will also get yourself into great shape.

1   What are the three main types of exercise, and what are some examples of each?

2   What is your opinion of doing exercise? How do you believe it can benefit people?

## Brainstorming

Think about the topic and brainstorm some ideas for your essay. Refer to the words and definitions below for help. Then, answer the questions

### Building Ideas

| How Can I Improve My Health? | | |
| --- | --- | --- |
| Change 1 | Change 2 | Change 3 |
| | | |

### Building Vocabulary

**exercise** *(v)* to do physical activity with the goal of improving one's body or having fun

**strength** *(n)* physical power

**physical fitness** *(n)* the act of having one's body be in good shape or condition

**active** *(adj)* doing various actions, often involving something physical; not being lazy

**inactive** *(adj)* not doing various actions, often involving something physical; being lazy

**discipline** *(n)* behavior on a regular basis that helps improve a skill or ability

**stamina** *(n)* physical strength or power; the ability to resist disease or various types of weaknesses

**routine** *(n)* a regular set of actions that a person does, often on a daily basis

**condition** *(n)* the state of a person's physical or mental health

**nutrition** *(n)* the act of taking in food that is good for one's body; good, healthy food

**diet** *(n)* the food that a person eats on a regular basis

**obese** *(adj)* very fat

**overweight** *(adj)* weighing too much; very fat

**underweight** *(adj)* not weighing enough; very thin or skinny

**weight watch** *(v)* to make sure that one's weight is under control and not too much or too little

**habit** *(n)* an activity that a person does on a regular basis

**stress** *(n)* mental or physical strain on one's body

**alcoholism** *(n)* the act of regularly drinking too much beer, wine, or other types of alcohol

**depression** *(n)* extreme sadness

**junk food** *(n)* unhealthy food, including potato chips, chocolate, and fast food, that is often cheap but delicious

**harmful** *(adj)* not good; causing damage, such as to one's body

**beneficial** *(adj)* good or helpful; improving something, such as one's body

**hygiene** *(n)* the act of keeping one's body clean

**immune system** *(n)* the part of the body that keeps it healthy and resists diseases

**recover** *(v)* to get better; to become healthier, often after being sick or unwell

**treat** *(v)* to attempt to heal a problem or to make a sick person better

*Fill in the blanks with the words above.*

1  Susan has an exercise _____ she follows each week.

2  You will be _____ if you fail to eat enough food.

*Choose the correct words for the sentences.*

3  She suffers from (alcoholism / depression) because she simply cannot be happy.

4  (Obese / Underweight) people can suffer health problems until they go on a diet.

## Making an Outline

Look at the ideas you came up with in the brainstorming section. Then, use them to create an outline for your essay.

| Introduction |
|---|

| Body |
|---|

| Detail 1 | Detail 2 | Detail 3 |
|---|---|---|

| Conclusion |
|---|

## First Draft

Use the outline you wrote above to write the first draft of your essay.

## Thesis and Topic Statements

All essays should include a thesis statement as well as topic statements. The thesis statement should appear in the introduction. There should be a topic statement in each body paragraph.

The thesis statement is one of the most important sentences in the entire essay. It explains the topic of the essay and what you will argue. It is crucial to make this sentence as clear as possible. Then, argue exactly that point. When you finish writing, review your thesis statement carefully to see if it matches your arguments in the essay.

You must include a topic statement in every body paragraph. In most cases, it is the first sentence in the paragraph. It should clearly state the main idea of the paragraph. Do not be vague; instead, be clear about your point. In addition, avoid making a topic statement too long. Shorter is better. Finally, be sure that every topic statement agrees with the thesis statement in order to have a strong essay.

**Model Essay**     Read the following sample essay. Underline the topic statements.

### How to Improve My Health

I am a healthy person in general. However, there are several ways I can improve my health. I will discuss three in this essay. The ways to improve my health are to change my eating habits, to exercise more, and to reduce my stress. Let me explain how I can do each of these activities.

First of all, I have to change my eating habits by consuming more nutritious food. Currently, I eat too much fast food and enjoy sugary snacks such as chocolate and candy bars. I ought to stop eating all of that junk food and start eating better food. I plan to eat more vegetables, especially leafy green ones like lettuce and broccoli. I must also eat more fruits, nuts, and healthy meats such as fish.

The next way I intend to improve my health is to exercise more often. I sometimes play sports at the park with my friends, but that is not sufficient. I should exercise for thirty minutes each day at least five days a week. I want to do a combination of exercises so that I can improve my strength and flexibility and enhance my cardiovascular system.

Finally, I absolutely must reduce the stress in my life. I am a student, so I study constantly and also worry about my grades all the time. To lower my stress level, I can do many things. I should get more sleep and meditate while I am awake. I should also try to have some fun by going out with my friends.

If I can do those three activities, I can improve my health a great deal. That will allow me to have a better, happier, and healthier life.

**Grammar in Writing**

Use "**have to + verb**" and "**must + verb**" to refer to activities that you are required to do. Use "**should + verb**" and "**ought to + verb**" to refer to activities that you are not required to do but are good ideas.

- I have to lose weight. → I must lose weight.

- John should eat more nutritious food. → John ought to eat more nutritious food.

*Write two sentences with "have to + verb" or "must + verb" and two sentences with "should + verb" or "ought to + verb."*

1 _____

2 _____

3 _____

4 _____

*Circle "have to + verb," "must + verb," "should + verb," and "ought to + verb" in the essay on the previous page.*

**Self-Evaluation**   Reread your first draft. Then, complete the following self-evaluation.

| | | | |
|---|---|---|---|
| 1 | Did I write a five-paragraph essay? | ☐ YES | ☐ NO |
| 2 | Did I include a thesis statement in the introduction? | ☐ YES | ☐ NO |
| 3 | Did I use examples in each body paragraph? | ☐ YES | ☐ NO |
| 4 | Did I include a topic statement in each body paragraph? | ☐ YES | ☐ NO |
| 5 | Did I restate the thesis statement in the conclusion? | ☐ YES | ☐ NO |
| 6 | Did I use correct grammar? | ☐ YES | ☐ NO |
| 7 | Did I use correct spelling? | ☐ YES | ☐ NO |
| 8 | Did I use correct punctuation? | ☐ YES | ☐ NO |
| 9 | Did I use sequence words properly? | ☐ YES | ☐ NO |
| 10 | Did I use transition words well? | ☐ YES | ☐ NO |
| 11 | Did I avoid using contractions? | ☐ YES | ☐ NO |
| 12 | Did I make logical arguments? | ☐ YES | ☐ NO |

**Final Draft**   Now, using the self-evaluation, write your final draft.

........................................................................................................................

........................................................................................................................

........................................................................................................................

........................................................................................................................

........................................................................................................................

........................................................................................................................

........................................................................................................................

........................................................................................................................

........................................................................................................................

........................................................................................................................

**Evaluate Your
Partner's Essay**   Read your partner's essay and make positive and negative comments on it. Use the self-evaluation form on the previous page if you need help.

**Choose the
Best Essay**   Divide into groups of four and read all of the essays. Then, decide which essay is the best. Discuss why you feel that way with your group members.

**More
Topics**

Look at the following topics. Choose one of them and write an expository essay.

- What are some bad habits that make people unhealthy?

- How does mental health affect people?

- What are some ways that people can improve their diets?

- What are some problems caused by poor health?

- How do people benefit from being healthy?

# 03
# How to Be a Good Friend

**WRITING ASSIGNMENT**  Think about your friendships with others. Do you consider yourself a good friend? In what ways can you become a better friend?

**Building Background**  Read the following website article. Then, answer the questions.

← → ↻ http://www.betterliving.com

## Positive Characteristics: **Survey Results**

*by Irene Davis*

Last month, *Better Living* magazine carried out an online survey of its readers, most of whom are between the ages of sixteen and seventy. It asked them to select what they believed the most important characteristics a person could have were. A list of ten words was provided. The words were kindness, imagination, determination, optimism, bravery, compassion, honor, loyalty, fairness, and tact. Survey takers were asked to rank all of the words on a scale from one to ten. They were not permitted to choose other words, but they were asked to leave comments.

The characteristic that came in number one overall was loyalty. 22% of the survey takers voted it for number one. One comment, by reader J. Sullivan, was, "A person needs to be loyal to himself and others. I can't imagine any other characteristics being more important than loyalty."

The second-most important characteristic was optimism. Roughly 14% of people selected it. Many comments about it were like the one submitted by T. Watson, who wrote, "Optimism is what helped humans fly to the moon and defeat all kinds of diseases. We believed we could do these things, so we did them."

Interestingly, the word that came in last in the survey was tact. Only 3% of the survey takers voted for it for the number-one position. "I don't want people to be tactful around me," wrote H. Harper. "I want them to tell me exactly what they're thinking. Let the diplomats worry about being tactful. But I want nothing to do with it."

1   What comments did people make about the characteristics?

2   Of the ten words listed, which is the most important in your opinion? Which is the least important? Why?

## Brainstorming

Think about the topic and brainstorm some ideas for your essay. Refer to the words and definitions below for help. Then, answer the questions.

### Building Ideas

| How Can I Be a Good Friend? | | |
| --- | --- | --- |
| Change 1 | Change 2 | Change 3 |
| | | |

### Building Vocabulary

**trust** *(v)* to believe or have faith in another person

**honesty** *(n)* the act of telling the truth and not lying

**keep a secret** *(phr)* not to tell one person's private information or stories to others

**tell a secret** *(phr)* to tell one person's private information or stories to another

**dependable** *(adj)* trustworthy; likely to do what one says one will do

**good listener** *(n)* a person who listens closely to what other people say

**poor listener** *(n)* a person who ignores others while talking or who does not want to listen to others

**forgive** *(v)* to pardon someone for an action, often negative, the person did in the past

**apologize** *(v)* to say that one is sorry for having done something

**silence** *(n)* quietness; the act of not talking or making noise

**loyalty** *(n)* the act of being faithful to someone or standing with that person, especially during hard times

**selfless** *(adj)* having little concern for one's self regarding money, fame, or position

**selfish** *(adj)* desiring more of things such as money, fame, and power

**use a person** *(phr)* to take advantage of a person

**respect** *(v)* to honor a person; to show great regard to a person

**disrespect** *(v)* to treat a person rudely or poorly

**favor** *(n)* an act someone does for another person out of niceness

**kindness** *(n)* the act of being friendly or nice

**warmhearted** *(adj)* having a kind or nice nature

**coldhearted** *(adj)* lacking kindness; being unfriendly toward others

**tactful** *(adj)* having the ability to say the right thing; being able to deal with sensitive situations well

**tactless** *(adj)* lacking the ability to say the right thing; making inappropriate comments at the wrong time

**keep in touch** *(phr)* to call, write, or communicate with someone, often while not being able to see that individual in person

**reach out** *(phr)* to make an attempt to communicate with someone or to be friendly to that person

### *Fill in the blanks with the words above.*

1  I asked my friend for a _____ , and he agreed to help me.

2  Sometimes _____ is much better than simply talking all the time.

### *Choose the correct words for the sentences.*

3  I cannot be friends with him because he cannot (keep a secret / tell a secret).

4  David is such a (coldhearted / warmhearted) person that everybody likes him.

**Making an Outline**   Look at the ideas you came up with in the brainstorming section. Then, use them to create an outline for your essay.

## Introduction

## Body

| Detail 1 | Detail 2 | Detail 3 |

## Conclusion

**First Draft**   Use the outline you wrote above to write the first draft of your essay.

## Writing an Introduction

The introduction is always the first paragraph in your essay. This makes it extremely important because it is the first thing you write that readers will see. You must therefore get readers interested in your essay, explain your thesis, and describe how you propose to defend your thesis in your introduction.

The first sentence should hook readers and make them want to read your essay. You can do this in many ways. These include asking a question, describing a touching event, or providing shocking statistics.

Next, write a thesis statement clearly explaining what you will argue in the essay. Make the thesis statement straightforward to avoid confusing readers. Then, mention the points you intend to make to defend your thesis.

Many essayists write the introduction after finishing the rest of their essay. This way, they know exactly what the thesis statement should be as well as which examples to write about. Try doing this the next time you write an essay.

**Model Essay** Read the following sample essay. Complete the introduction to the essay by using the information in the passage above.

## How to Be a Good Friend

Have you ever wondered how to be a good friend? I used to be friendless, and it really bothered me. _____ .

For me, being a good listener, being trustworthy, and engaging in give and take were vital to becoming a good friend.

People love talking about themselves, so a good friend should be a good listener. I was once a big talker who loved telling people about myself, but nobody wanted to listen to me. When I started being quiet and listening to others, I acquired more friends. Few people listen well, so good listeners are highly valued as friends.

Next, it is crucial to be a trustworthy person. I lost countless friends in the past because I could not keep their secrets. If somebody told me a secret, I immediately blabbed about it to others. I realized I had to become more trustworthy. People learned they could speak to me in confidence, and I would not tell others anything.

Finally, there must be give and take for a relationship to be successful. When people did favors for me, I never returned their kindness. But friends do not act that way, so I changed my ways. Now, when a friend does something nice for me, I return the favor by doing something nice for that friend.

Being a good friend is not difficult. You simply need to listen to others and avoid talking about yourself too much. In addition, be trustworthy and engage in give and take. Follow those three simple steps, and you can be a good friend.

## Grammar in Writing

Use "**when**" to talk about two activities, actions, or situations that happen at the same time. Put "when" in front of one sentence to connect it to another. If you use "when" at the beginning of a sentence, add a comma (,) before the second sentence begins.

- When you are a trustworthy person, you will have many friends. → You will have many friends when you are a trustworthy person.

- When she started listening well, people liked her. → People liked her when she started listening well.

*Write two sentences with "when" at the beginning of the sentence and two sentences with "when" in the middle of the sentence.*

1 _____

2 _____

3 _____

4 _____

*Circle "when" in the essay on the previous page.*

## Self-Evaluation    Reread your first draft. Then, complete the following self-evaluation.

| | | | |
|---|---|---|---|
| 1 | Did I write a five-paragraph essay? | ☐ YES | ☐ NO |
| 2 | Did I include a thesis statement in the introduction? | ☐ YES | ☐ NO |
| 3 | Did I use examples in each body paragraph? | ☐ YES | ☐ NO |
| 4 | Did I include a topic statement in each body paragraph? | ☐ YES | ☐ NO |
| 5 | Did I restate the thesis statement in the conclusion? | ☐ YES | ☐ NO |
| 6 | Did I use correct grammar? | ☐ YES | ☐ NO |
| 7 | Did I use correct spelling? | ☐ YES | ☐ NO |
| 8 | Did I use correct punctuation? | ☐ YES | ☐ NO |
| 9 | Did I use sequence words properly? | ☐ YES | ☐ NO |
| 10 | Did I use transition words well? | ☐ YES | ☐ NO |
| 11 | Did I avoid using contractions? | ☐ YES | ☐ NO |
| 12 | Did I make logical arguments? | ☐ YES | ☐ NO |

**Final Draft**    Now, using the self-evaluation, write your final draft.

**Evaluate Your Partner's Essay**    Read your partner's essay and make positive and negative comments on it. Use the self-evaluation form on the previous page if you need help.

**Choose the Best Essay**    Divide into groups of four and read all of the essays. Then, decide which essay is the best. Discuss why you feel that way with your group members.

Look at the following topics. Choose one of them and write an expository essay.

- What characteristics do you admire in other people?

- Why do people need friends?

- How can friends help one another?

- How can you change your bad habits to make yourself a better friend?

- What characteristics in your friends do you dislike the most?

**More Topics**

# 04 The Water Cycle

**WRITING ASSIGNMENT**

What is the water cycle? Do you know the different stages of it? Why is the water cycle important to the Earth?

## Building Background

Read the following newspaper article. Then, answer the questions.

## Water Erosion

*by Keith Jackson*

Water ranks among the most important of all substances on the Earth. Without it, plants and animals could not survive. Water covers more than 2/3 of the Earth's surface. It is also responsible for changing the appearance of the land. It does this through a process known as erosion.

Erosion refers to the wearing away of the land through natural processes. Erosion can happen in a number of ways, both natural and manmade. These include wind, ice, temperature, and gravity. But water erosion is the most common and powerful of all the types of erosion.

Water erosion can change the face of the land very quickly or extremely slowly. When storms cause water levels to rise and to flood the land, water erosion tends to happen quickly.

Floodwaters from hurricanes and typhoons can wash away large amounts of soil while uprooting trees and other plants. As a result, when the waters recede, erosion can have occurred in a matter of days or even hours.

On the other hand, water erosion can take millions of years to change the face of the Earth's surface. The Grand Canyon in Arizona, USA, was carved out through the forces of water erosion. Over a period lasting around thirty-five million years ago, the water in the Colorado River slowly washed away the land. This resulted in the formation of the Grand Canyon, which is around 1,800 meters deep in some places. In fact, water erosion continues at the Grand Canyon to this day. In another million years or two, the canyon will be even deeper than it is today.

1 What is an example of water erosion happening quickly? What is an example of it happening more slowly?

2 How do you think that water erosion can harm the land? Can you think of any recent instances when water erosion has changed the appearance of the land where you live?

**Brainstorming** Think about the topic and brainstorm some ideas for your essay. Refer to the words and definitions below for help. Then, answer the questions.

**Building Ideas**

## The Water Cycle

| Stage 1 | Stage 2 | Stage 3 |
|---|---|---|
| | | |

**Building Vocabulary**

**evaporate** *(v)* to change from a liquid to a gas

**gaseous** *(adj)* relating to gas

**body of water** *(n)* any large area of water such as an ocean, sea, river, or lake

**ecosystem** *(n)* an area that includes the living and nonliving elements in it and their interactions

**aquatic** *(adj)* relating to water

**water vapor** *(n)* water in its gaseous form

**stage** *(n)* a step; one part of a process

**droplet** *(n)* a tiny bit of a liquid such as water

**purify** *(v)* to make something clean

**atmosphere** *(n)* the air

**cloud** *(n)* a collection of visible particles of water in the air

**condense** *(v)* to change from a gas into a liquid or solid

**temperature** *(n)* how hot or cold something is

**particle** *(n)* a small piece of something

**dust** *(n)* a tiny piece of dirt or other type of fine particle

**accumulate** *(v)* to gather; to collect

**saturate** *(v)* to soak or fill completely

**precipitation** *(n)* water in any form that falls from the sky to the ground

**hail** *(n)* small pellets of ice that may fall to the ground

**sleet** *(n)* a combination of ice and freezing rain that may fall to the ground

**collection** *(n)* the act of water gathering in oceans, seas, rivers, and lakes

**runoff** *(n)* rainfall that does not soak into the ground

**groundwater** *(n)* water that is located beneath the surface of the Earth in the ground

**distribute** *(v)* to spread or scatter over a wide area

*Fill in the blanks with the words above.*

1   It is important to _____ the water before you drink it.

2   The heavy snow is starting to _____ on the ground.

*Choose the correct words for the sentences.*

3   Deserts get a tiny amount of (precipitation / collection) annually.

4   Water droplets in the air often attach themselves to small particles of (dust / hail).

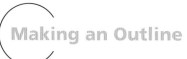

## Making an Outline

Look at the ideas you came up with in the brainstorming section. Then, use them to create an outline for your essay.

### Introduction

### Body

| Detail 1 | Detail 2 | Detail 3 |
| --- | --- | --- |
| | | |

### Conclusion

## First Draft

Use the outline you wrote above to write the first draft of your essay.

## Writing a Conclusion

The conclusion is always the last paragraph in your essay. This makes it extremely important because it is your last opportunity to convince your readers of the point you are making in your essay. You must therefore restate your thesis statement, provide a short summary with examples, and write a concluding statement.

The first sentence in the conclusion should indicate to readers that your essay is about to end. You can do this by mentioning your thesis statement and indicating that you have proven it.

Next, provide a short summary of the body paragraphs in your essay. You do not need to go into too much detail, but you can provide an example or two from the essay.

Finally, write a concluding statement that sums up your essay. Try to include a clever, funny, or thought-provoking comment, an important statistic, or a question that will make your reader think about what you wrote in your essay.

Read the following sample essay. Complete the conclusion to the essay by using the information in the passage above.

## The Water Cycle

The water cycle refers to the circulation of water in its solid, liquid, and gaseous forms around the Earth. Because water is vital to all life, a thorough understanding of the water cycle is important. There are four basic steps involved in it: evaporation, condensation, precipitation, and collection.

When water evaporates, it changes from a liquid into its gaseous form, called water vapor. Evaporation takes place due to the sun's heat. Heat from the sun causes water in various bodies of water to evaporate.

Water vapor is so small that people cannot see it. Water vapor slowly rises into the air. At some point, the air temperature becomes cold enough that water vapor changes into liquid form once again. This is called condensation. When water condenses, there are small droplets of water in the air. They often combine to form clouds.

The next stage is precipitation. When clouds release the water in them, it falls to the ground as rain, snow, sleet, hail, or ice. This water may be absorbed into the ground. It may also fall into oceans, seas, rivers, lakes, and other bodies of water and be collected there. This is the final stage of the water cycle. Once collection occurs, evaporation can take place, and the cycle begins again.

_____

_____ .

The water cycle never ends and constantly takes place.

**Grammar in Writing**

*A*, *an*, and *the* are articles in English. *A* and *an* are indefinite articles. Use them to refer to something in general. *The* is a definite article. Use it to refer to something specific. You cannot use *a* and *an* with uncountable nouns. You can only use them with countable nouns. *The* can be used with countable and uncountable nouns.

- Rain is a form of precipitation.
- Rain is the main form of precipitation here.

- They will visit a lake this weekend.
- They will visit the lake near their home this weekend.

*Write two sentences with either "a" or "an" in front of a noun. Then, write two sentences with "the" in front of a noun.*

1 _____

2 _____

3 _____

4 _____

*Circle the articles in the essay on the previous page.*

**Self-Evaluation**    Reread your first draft. Then, complete the following self-evaluation.

| | | | |
|---|---|---|---|
| 1 | Did I write a five-paragraph essay? | ☐ YES | ☐ NO |
| 2 | Did I include a thesis statement in the introduction? | ☐ YES | ☐ NO |
| 3 | Did I use examples in each body paragraph? | ☐ YES | ☐ NO |
| 4 | Did I include a topic statement in each body paragraph? | ☐ YES | ☐ NO |
| 5 | Did I restate the thesis statement in the conclusion? | ☐ YES | ☐ NO |
| 6 | Did I use correct grammar? | ☐ YES | ☐ NO |
| 7 | Did I use correct spelling? | ☐ YES | ☐ NO |
| 8 | Did I use correct punctuation? | ☐ YES | ☐ NO |
| 9 | Did I use sequence words properly? | ☐ YES | ☐ NO |
| 10 | Did I use transition words well? | ☐ YES | ☐ NO |
| 11 | Did I avoid using contractions? | ☐ YES | ☐ NO |
| 12 | Did I make logical arguments? | ☐ YES | ☐ NO |

**Final Draft**   Now, using the self-evaluation, write your final draft.

**Evaluate Your Partner's Essay**   Read your partner's essay and make positive and negative comments on it. Use the self-evaluation form on the previous page if you need help.

**Choose the Best Essay**   Divide into groups of four and read all of the essays. Then, decide which essay is the best. Discuss why you feel that way with your group members.

Look at the following topics. Choose one of them and write an expository essay.

**More Topics**

- What are some different types of erosion?

- How does photosynthesis take place?

- What are the differences between various types of bodies of water?

- How do plants and animals use water?

- What is the food chain?

# UNIT

# 05 How to Make Your Favorite Food

**WRITING ASSIGNMENT** What is your favorite food? Do you know how to make it? Can you explain all of the steps that are necessary to make it?

**Building Background** Read the following magazine article. Then, answer the questions.

## Dry-Heat and Moist-Heat Cooking

**Writer** *Jessica West*

There are numerous ways to cook food. The majority can be placed into two different categories: dry-heat cooking and moist-heat cooking.

Dry-heat cooking uses either the air or fat for cooking. Baking, frying, sautéing, grilling, roasting, and broiling are dry-heat cooking methods. These methods involve the browning of food and create flavor by caramelizing it. Roasting and baking utilize an oven. They use air to transfer heat, which cooks food. Sautéing is done on a stove and employs high heat and little oil. Frying requires more oil than sautéing. In the case of deep-frying, food is completely covered in oil and cooked. Grilling is a popular method for cooking meat such as steaks, hamburgers, and ribs. It is often done on a grill or cast-iron surface. For grilling, food is cooked by a flame or heat source beneath the food. Broiling is similar to grilling but involves using heat from an overhead source.

Moist-heat cooking requires the use of water or steam to cook food. The four most common moist-heat cooking methods are boiling, simmering, poaching, and steaming. Boiling involves cooking food in water at the highest possible temperature, which is 100 degrees Celsius. Pasta is often cooked in boiling water. Simmering, which is used for stews and soups, requires cooking food in water between 85 and 96 degrees Celsius. Poaching involves cooking food in water between 71 and 82 degrees. Eggs are frequently poached. To steam food, water is boiled, and then the steam rising from the water cooks the food. This method cooks food quickly and is often used for vegetables.

1 What are the two main categories of cooking? Which cooking methods can be placed in each category?

2 What types of foods do you cook? How do you cook them?

**Brainstorming** Think about the topic and brainstorm some ideas for your essay. Refer to the words and definitions below for help. Then, answer the questions.

## Building Ideas

| How to Make My Favorite Food | | |
|---|---|---|
| Step 1 | Step 2 | Step 3 |
| | | |

## Building Vocabulary

**ingredient** (n) something that is added to a mixture

**spice** (n) a type of strong-smelling or tasting plant, such as pepper, cinnamon, or basil, that is put in or on food to improve its taste

**add** (v) to put something into a mixture

**mix** (v) to combine two or more things with one another

**stir** (v) to use a spoon or other utensil to mix something together

**whisk** (v) to stir rapidly, often in a circular motion

**preheat** (v) to turn on an oven so that it will reach a desired temperature for cooking

**fry** (v) to cook food by using oil in a pan on a stove

**boil** (v) to heat water to 100 degrees Celsius so that bubbles are created in the water

**simmer** (v) to heat water to a level just beneath its boiling point

**sauté** (v) to cook food on a stove by using high heat and little oil

**bake** (v) to roast food in an oven

**caramelize** (v) to cook food so that it becomes like caramel and is brown and chewy

**slice** (v) to cut into pieces

**mince** (v) to cut into very small pieces

**puree** (v) to put a food mixture into a blender

**crockpot** (n) a slow cooker; an electric pot that cooks food at low temperatures for several hours

**tenderize** (v) to make something such as meat soft or tender

**steam** (v) to boil water and then to use the steam created from the water to cook food

**melt** (v) to change from a solid to a liquid state

**undercook** (v) not to cook something enough

**overcook** (v) to cook something too long

**burn** (v) to cook food so much that it becomes black in color

**barbecue** (v) to grill food; to cook food such as meat outdoors on an open flame

*Fill in the blanks with the words above.*

1   You have to _____ the flour, eggs, and sugar with a spoon to combine everything.

2   We put the food in the _____ and then let it cook all day long.

*Choose the correct words for the sentences.*

3   If you (undercook / overcook) chicken, you could get sick because the food will not be safe to eat.

4   Please (mince / slice) the cake into ten small pieces.

## Making an Outline
Look at the ideas you came up with in the brainstorming section. Then, use them to create an outline for your essay.

| Introduction |
|---|
| |

| Body | | |
|---|---|---|
| Detail 1 | Detail 2 | Detail 3 |
| | | |

| Conclusion |
|---|
| |

## First Draft
Use the outline you wrote above to write the first draft of your essay.

## Sequence Words

When you describe an event, tell a story, or give directions or instructions, there are normally several steps in the process. You should therefore use sequence words to make your writing clearer because they let the reader follow the event, story, directions, or instructions more easily.

There are a wide variety of sequence words you can use. In many cases, it is easy to use ordinal numbers when listing steps. So simply use words such as *first, second, third, fourth,* and *fifth* until you list every step involved.

There are other sequence words as well. When starting a sequence, most people use *first, firstly, first of all,* or *to begin with*. For the other steps, people often use *now, then, next,* and *after that*. For the final step, people may use *last, lastly, last of all,* or *finally*.

Use sequence words at the beginnings of sentences. In addition, put a comma (,) after each sequence word when you write it.

## Model Essay

Read the following sample essay. Fill in the blanks with appropriate sequence words.

### How to Make My Favorite Food

There are many foods I like, but my favorite food is pork chops with baked apples. It sounds complicated, but it is actually easy to make. There are only a few simple steps you need to follow.

(1) _____ , you need to prepare your ingredients. To make this meal, you need four pork chops, two apples, and some raisins. You must also have salt, brown sugar, cinnamon, cloves, and apple juice. In addition, you need a baking pan coated in oil, and you should heat the oven to 350 degrees Celsius.

(2) _____ , peel the apples, slice them, and put them into the baking pan. (3) _____ , put a handful of raisins on top of the apples. (4) _____ , sprinkle some brown sugar, cinnamon, and cloves on the apples and raisins. (5) _____ , put some salt on the pork chops and place them on the apples. (6) _____ , put the pan into the oven and bake for around forty minutes.

(7) _____ , you need to make the sauce. Pour some apple juice and brown sugar into a pan. Heat it to a boil and then simmer it for about ten minutes. When the pork chops are done, you can pour the sauce on them, or you can dip the pork chops or apples into the sauce.

Pork chops and apples is my favorite food, and it is not difficult to cook. Just prepare the ingredients, put the spices on the pork and apples, and cook everything in the oven. When the food is finished, you can enjoy a delicious meal.

**Grammar in Writing**

A series is three or more words, phrases, or sentences that combine to create a list. When making a series, separate the words, phrases, or sentences with commas. Use **"and"** before the last part of the series. So use A, B, and C or A, B, C, and D. In addition, make sure that everything in the series uses the same part of speech. So use *noun, noun, and noun, verb, verb, and verb,* or *sentence, sentence, and sentence.*

- To make a cake, you need butter, flour, **and** sugar.
- The chef enjoys frying, baking, **and** grilling food.
- You should put the food in the oven, cook it for twenty minutes, **and** then let it cool.

*Write two sentences using words in a series and two sentences using phrases or sentences in a series.*

1 

2 

3 

4 

*Circle all of the examples of a series in the essay on the previous page.*

**Self-Evaluation**   Reread your first draft. Then, complete the following self-evaluation.

| | | | |
|---|---|---|---|
| 1 | Did I write a five-paragraph essay? | ☐ YES | ☐ NO |
| 2 | Did I include a thesis statement in the introduction? | ☐ YES | ☐ NO |
| 3 | Did I use examples in each body paragraph? | ☐ YES | ☐ NO |
| 4 | Did I include a topic statement in each body paragraph? | ☐ YES | ☐ NO |
| 5 | Did I restate the thesis statement in the conclusion? | ☐ YES | ☐ NO |
| 6 | Did I use correct grammar? | ☐ YES | ☐ NO |
| 7 | Did I use correct spelling? | ☐ YES | ☐ NO |
| 8 | Did I use correct punctuation? | ☐ YES | ☐ NO |
| 9 | Did I use sequence words properly? | ☐ YES | ☐ NO |
| 10 | Did I use transition words well? | ☐ YES | ☐ NO |
| 11 | Did I avoid using contractions? | ☐ YES | ☐ NO |
| 12 | Did I make logical arguments? | ☐ YES | ☐ NO |

**Final Draft**   Now, using the self-evaluation, write your final draft.

**Evaluate Your Partner's Essay**   Read your partner's essay and make positive and negative comments on it. Use the self-evaluation form on the previous page if you need help.

**Choose the Best Essay**   Divide into groups of four and read all of the essays. Then, decide which essay is the best. Discuss why you feel that way with your group members.

Look at the following topics. Choose one of them and write an expository essay.

**More Topics**

- How can you get to your favorite restaurant?

- What are the health benefits of your favorite food?

- What is your favorite cooking method, and what foods do you cook that way?

- What are some unhealthy foods, and why are they unhealthy?

- What nutrients should people try to eat every day?

# Descriptive Writing

The purpose of **descriptive writing** is to provide a vivid image of a person, place, or thing in the reader's mind. Descriptive writing should focus on what something looks like and should enable the reader to get a good sense of the topic about which the person is writing. The reader should be able clearly to imagine the topic of the essay merely by reading the words in it. This type of writing is found in travel guides and pamphlets. It can also be found in art books as well as other academic works.

A work of descriptive writing needs a strong thesis statement to indicate what the precise topic of the essay will be. The essay should then contain body paragraphs which describe the topic of the essay as precisely as possible. The conclusion should then provide a summary of what was described in the body paragraphs.

Here are some examples of descriptive writing.

**Example 1**
My favorite restaurant is a buffet restaurant which is located about ten minutes away from my home. The restaurant has numerous tables and a couple of private rooms that are used for big events. There are several different stations filled with all kinds of foods from around the world. Some of the food that is served there includes seafood, beef, chicken, pork, numerous vegetables, pasta dishes, pizza, and breads. There are also a wide variety of desserts and beverages for diners to choose from.

**Example 2**
My grandfather is around 175 centimeters tall and has short white hair. He has brown eyes and a straight nose. He sometimes walks bent over because he is getting old. You can always see him wearing glasses since his eyesight is not as good as it used to be. He prefers to wear formal clothes, so he often wears a suit and tie despite the fact that he no longer works. He also likes wearing hats because he believes they make him look stylish. He typically wears dark colors such as black or gray, but he likes colorful ties.

# 06 Your Favorite Painting

**WRITING ASSIGNMENT**  What is your favorite painting? Who painted it, and what does it look like? Can you describe how your favorite painting looks?

**Building Background**  Read the following announcement. Then, answer the questions.

## New Art Gallery to Open

This Saturday, the Johnston Art Gallery is going to open its doors for the first time. Located at 98 Claymore Avenue, the gallery will be exhibiting more than 200 works of art. This Saturday only, admission to the gallery will be free to all visitors.

For its first exhibition, the gallery will display more than 50 works created by Renaissance masters. This temporary exhibit will have works by Botticelli, Titian, Donatello, Michelangelo, Leonardo da Vinci, and other notable names.

There will be several still-life paintings by French Impressionists on display as well as some landscape works by American artists from the Hudson River School of the nineteenth century. The remaining paintings that will be exhibited will be portraits and watercolors by local artists. All of those paintings will be available for purchase.

Finally, the gallery will be registering budding young artists for classes. At these classes, students can learn how to paint in a wide variety of styles and create art with both oil paints and watercolors.

For more information, call 844-0328 and ask for Susan.

1   What types of artwork will be on display at the gallery?

2   Which works of art at the gallery would you like to see the most? Why do you feel that way?

# Brainstorming

Think about the topic and brainstorm some ideas for your essay. Refer to the words and definitions below for help. Then, answer the questions.

## Building Ideas

| What is Your Favorite Painting? | | |
| --- | --- | --- |
| Artist and Type of Work | Appearance | Unique Points and Interpretation |
| | | |

## Building Vocabulary

**realist art** (n) a style of art in which figures and scenes appear as they do in real life

**abstract art** (n) a style of art in which figures and scenes do not resemble reality

**impressionism** (n) a style of art in which figures and scenes appear according to the artist's impression of them

**period** (n) a specific era or time

**master painter** (n) an artist who is considered great at creating paintings

**masterpiece** (n) an outstanding work of art

**brushstroke** (n) the movement of a paintbrush

**landscape** (n) a painting of a scene from nature

**portrait** (n) a painting of an individual

**still-life** (n) a painting of inanimate objects, such as fruit in a bowl

**perspective** (n) the method of showing three-dimensional objects and special relationships on a flat surface

**technique** (n) a method or way of doing something

**translucent** (adj) clear; letting light pass through

**opaque** (adj) unclear; not letting light pass through

**gesture** (n) a movement of the arms, legs, head, or other body part that has a particular meaning or shows a certain emotion

**vibrant** (adj) bright; alive

**dull** (adj) not bright; dark

**obscure** (adj) difficult to see

**compose** (v) to make or create

**imagine** (v) to think of something new

**creative** (adj) having the ability to make new things or ideas

**reflect** (v) to show; to reproduce

**primary color** (n) red, yellow, or blue

**secondary color** (n) a color obtained by mixing two primary ones: orange, green, or purple

**tertiary color** (n) a color obtained by mixing a primary color with a secondary one

**hue** (n) a color

*Fill in the blanks with the words above.*

1   The artist uses long _____ to give his paintings a unique appearance.

2   Her _____ mind let her make many unique pictures.

*Choose the correct words for the sentences.*

3   Michelangelo is a considered a (masterpiece / master painter) by most people.

4   Orange is one of the three (primary colors / secondary colors).

## Making an Outline

Look at the ideas you came up with in the brainstorming section. Then, use them to create an outline for your essay.

### Introduction

### Body

| Detail 1 | Detail 2 | Detail 3 |
| --- | --- | --- |

### Conclusion

## First Draft

Use the outline you wrote above to write the first draft of your essay.

## Formal and Informal Writing

All writing is either formal or informal. Formal writing is used in academic and work settings while people use informal writing to communicate with their friends or family members. When writing an essay, it is better to use formal writing on most occasions.

When writing formally, there are several things to avoid. First, do not use contractions. For example, instead of using *don't*, *can't*, or *shouldn't*, write *do not*, *cannot*, or *should not*. In addition, never use *wanna*, *gonna*, *hafta*, or other similar constructions. These are not words and should always be avoided in formal writing.

Formal writing also utilizes the passive voice rather than the active voice. So instead of writing, "You can see this painting," you should write, "This painting can be seen," in a formal essay. Finally, avoid clichés and colloquial words or expressions, such as *awesome*, *cool*, and *wow*, in formal writing. Only use them in informal writing.

Read the following sample essay. Underline the informal words and expressions and then think of how to rewrite them.

### My Favorite Painting

The title of my favorite painting is *Son of Man*. It's a work of surrealism that was painted by René Magritte in 1964. The painting is totally awesome, and that is what makes it my favorite work of art.

The painting depicts a man standing in front of a stone wall. He's wearing a gray overcoat as well as a bowler hat, a white shirt, and a red tie. Behind the wall, there is a body of water that looks like a sea or ocean, and there's also a cloudy sky.

Those features are not what make the painting interesting though. What I find fascinating about it is that we cannot see the man's face clearly because there is a green apple obscuring his face. The apple and some leaves are covering most of his face, so we cannot see who the man is.

If you look closely, you will notice that you can see part of the man's eyes peeking out around the apple. In addition, the man's arm appears to be bending backward rather than forward. According to Magritte, *Son of Man* is a self-portrait. However, because the man's face cannot be seen, it might not really be Magritte. It could be anyone hiding behind the apple, and that's why I love this painting.

*Son of Man* by René Magritte is my favorite painting. I really wanna see this painting in real life because of how mysterious and intriguing it is.

**Grammar in Writing**

Use "**because**" to connect to clauses to one another. Use "**because of + noun**" to connect a noun phrase with a sentence. When using "because" or "because of," there should be a cause/effect pattern in the sentence.

- **Because** I like paintings, I will go to the gallery. → I will go to the gallery **because** I like paintings.

- **Because of** the art class, I learned to paint well. → I learned to paint well **because of** the art class.

*Write two sentences with "because" and two sentences with "because of + noun."*

1 _____

2 _____

3 _____

4 _____

*Circle "because" and "because of" in the essay on the previous page.*

**Self-Evaluation**  Reread your first draft. Then, complete the following self-evaluation.

| | | | |
|---|---|---|---|
| 1 | Did I write a five-paragraph essay? | ☐ YES | ☐ NO |
| 2 | Did I include a thesis statement in the introduction? | ☐ YES | ☐ NO |
| 3 | Did I use examples in each body paragraph? | ☐ YES | ☐ NO |
| 4 | Did I include a topic statement in each body paragraph? | ☐ YES | ☐ NO |
| 5 | Did I restate the thesis statement in the conclusion? | ☐ YES | ☐ NO |
| 6 | Did I use correct grammar? | ☐ YES | ☐ NO |
| 7 | Did I use correct spelling? | ☐ YES | ☐ NO |
| 8 | Did I use correct punctuation? | ☐ YES | ☐ NO |
| 9 | Did I use sequence words properly? | ☐ YES | ☐ NO |
| 10 | Did I use transition words well? | ☐ YES | ☐ NO |
| 11 | Did I avoid using contractions? | ☐ YES | ☐ NO |
| 12 | Did I make logical arguments? | ☐ YES | ☐ NO |

## Final Draft

Now, using the self-evaluation, write your final draft.

_____

_____

_____

_____

_____

_____

_____

_____

_____

_____

_____

## Evaluate Your Partner's Essay

Read your partner's essay and make positive and negative comments on it. Use the self-evaluation form on the previous page if you need help.

## Choose the Best Essay

Divide into groups of four and read all of the essays. Then, decide which essay is the best. Discuss why you feel that way with your group members.

### More Topics

Look at the following topics. Choose one of them and write a descriptive essay.

- What is your favorite movie?

- Can you describe the events in the last work of fiction you read?

- What does a work of art that you created look like?

- What is a famous national treasure in your country?

- Can you describe an item on display in a museum in your city?

# 07 The Rooms in Your Home

**WRITING ASSIGNMENT**  Think about your home. How many rooms are in it? What rooms are there? Can you describe what these rooms look like and what is in them?

## Building Background    Read the following advertisement. Then, answer the questions.

Hampton Realty
**Let us find your next dream home**

We at Hampton Realty have more than 50 years of experience finding homes for people in the Springfield area. Take a look at some of the newest residences we have for sale.

**57 Brentwood Avenue**: 2-story home with 4 bedrooms, 3 bathrooms, large kitchen w/granite counters, spacious living room, 2-car garage, $210,000

**110 Morgan Road**: 2 bedrooms, 1 bathroom, kitchen, living room, small backyard, perfect for a young couple w/1 or no children, quiet neighborhood, $150,000

**75 Brandywine Street**: 3 bedrooms, 2 bathrooms, small kitchen, large dining room, huge living room w/fireplace, on-street parking, fenced-in backyard, near elementary and middle school, completely furnished, renters only, $2,500/month

**32 Watson Drive**: located on 12th floor of new apartment complex, 3 bedrooms, 2 bathrooms, living room, modernized kitchen w/built-in appliances, great view of downtown, 10-minute walk from subway station, $250,000

**27 Cedar Road**: 1 room in shared home; access to kitchen, bathroom, living room, free Wi-Fi, must pay share of utilities, including electricity, gas, and water, $300/month rent

Call us at 498-2827 to set up an appointment to visit one of these places or many of the others we have available. Go to www.hamptonrealty.com/availablehomes to find your next residence.

1  Can you describe all of the homes that are for sale? What is unique about them?

2  Which of the available homes would you prefer to rent or buy? Why would you like to live in that particular home?

**Brainstorming** Think about the topic and brainstorm some ideas for your essay. Refer to the words and definitions below for help. Then, answer the questions.

## Building Ideas

| The Rooms in My Home | | |
| --- | --- | --- |
| My Room | My Parents' and Siblings' Rooms | The Other Rooms |
| | | |

## Building Vocabulary

**apartment complex** *(n)* an area that has several apartment buildings located close to one another

**bedroom** *(n)* a room in which a person sleeps

**wardrobe** *(n)* a large piece of furniture in which one hangs clothes

**dresser** *(n)* a piece of furniture used to keep underwear, socks, and folded clothes in

**decorate** *(v)* to make a room look nicer, often by putting up pictures, paintings, or other similar things

**hang** *(v)* to suspend something in the air, such as by using a nail or a clothes hanger

**closet** *(n)* a small room that is used to store clothes and other items in

**kitchen** *(n)* a room in which food is kept and cooking is done

**cabinet** *(n)* a piece of furniture with shelves used for storing items

**appliance** *(n)* a piece of equipment that does some type of work

**living room** *(n)* a room in which people may relax and watch television

**couch** *(n)* a sofa

**coffee table** *(n)* a small table which people may put reading material or cups on

**dining room** *(n)* a room in which people eat their meals

**cozy** *(adj)* creating a pleasant feeling

**comfortable** *(adj)* making a person feel good or at ease

**ornament** *(n)* a decoration

**den** *(n)* a family room

**safe** *(n)* a heavy strongbox with a lock that people put valuable items inside

**cramped** *(adj)* not having much room or space

**office** *(n)* a room in which a person does work

**bathroom** *(n)* a room in which a person may take a shower or use the toilet

**basement** *(n)* a room which is found underground

**dark** *(adj)* not having much or any light

**bright** *(adj)* having a lot of light

**stuffy** *(adj)* difficult to breathe

**share** *(v)* to use something together with another person

*Fill in the blanks with the words above.*

1    There are several electric _____ in the kitchen.

2    She folds up most of her clothes and keeps them in her _____ .

*Choose the correct words for the sentences.*

3    The (basement / den) is dark since it is entirely underground.

4    I feel (cozy / cramped) in the bedroom I share with my two brothers.

## Making an Outline

Look at the ideas you came up with in the brainstorming section. Then, use them to create an outline for your essay.

**Introduction**

**Body**

Detail 1                    Detail 2                    Detail 3

**Conclusion**

## First Draft

Use the outline you wrote above to write the first draft of your essay.

**How to Make Your Writing Better**

## Transition Words

When you change from one topic to another in your essay, you are making a transition. To make these changes as smooth as possible, you should use transition words.

To show agreement or similarity in your transition, you can use words like *in addition, and, also, too, then, furthermore, as well*, and *additionally*. To show contrast or opposition, try using words such as *however, but, on the other hand, while, nevertheless, even so*, and *in contrast*.

To give examples or to provide support, transition words such as *for example, for instance, in fact, to demonstrate, as for, for this reason*, and *as an illustration* are ideal.

And to show an effect, result, or consequence, you can use transition words such as *therefore, consequently, thus, as a result, for this reason*, and *accordingly*.

In most cases, the transition word should start the sentence and should be followed by a comma. However, do not start a sentence with *also*. It should come after the subject.

**Model Essay**   Read the following sample essay. Underline the transition words.

### The Rooms in My Home

I live in a three-bedroom apartment with my family. Not only are there the three bedrooms, but my home contains a living room, a kitchen, and two bathrooms. Each room has its own special appearance and unique characteristics.

My bedroom is the smallest of the three bedrooms in my home. The major pieces of furniture in it are my bed, my desk, and my wardrobe. There is a large window overlooking a park, too. There are also a few posters of my favorite pop groups hanging on the walls.

The other two bedrooms belong to my parents and my older sister. While my parents' bedroom only has a bed and a wardrobe, my sister's bedroom has a desk like mine. Both of those bedrooms have pictures hanging from the walls as well.

As for the other rooms in my house, there is nothing special about the bathrooms. Each contains a sink, a toilet, and a shower. The kitchen also resembles a standard one in most people's homes. There are several appliances, including a stove, a microwave oven, a coffeemaker, and a refrigerator. The living room is comfortable and spacious. There is a large sofa big enough for everyone in my family, and there is a big-screen TV on the wall. Finally, there is a table where we eat our meals.

My home has lots of furniture and other items found in most people's homes. While there is nothing particularly special about my home, I think it looks great and love living there.

**Grammar in Writing**

Use "**there is**" and "**there are**" to say that something exists. Use "there is" with a singular noun or uncountable noun. And use "there are" with a plural noun. If there is a plural subject, even if each noun is singular, use "there are."

- There is a sofa in the bedroom.
- There are four people in my family.
- There is some sugar in the bowl.
- There are a refrigerator and a stove in my kitchen.

*Write two sentences with "there is" and two sentences with "there are."*

1 _____

2 _____

3 _____

4 _____

*Circle "there is" and "there are" in the essay on the previous page.*

**Self-Evaluation**   Reread your first draft. Then, complete the following self-evaluation.

| | | | |
|---|---|---|---|
| 1 | Did I write a five-paragraph essay? | ☐ YES | ☐ NO |
| 2 | Did I include a thesis statement in the introduction? | ☐ YES | ☐ NO |
| 3 | Did I use examples in each body paragraph? | ☐ YES | ☐ NO |
| 4 | Did I include a topic statement in each body paragraph? | ☐ YES | ☐ NO |
| 5 | Did I restate the thesis statement in the conclusion? | ☐ YES | ☐ NO |
| 6 | Did I use correct grammar? | ☐ YES | ☐ NO |
| 7 | Did I use correct spelling? | ☐ YES | ☐ NO |
| 8 | Did I use correct punctuation? | ☐ YES | ☐ NO |
| 9 | Did I use sequence words properly? | ☐ YES | ☐ NO |
| 10 | Did I use transition words well? | ☐ YES | ☐ NO |
| 11 | Did I avoid using contractions? | ☐ YES | ☐ NO |
| 12 | Did I make logical arguments? | ☐ YES | ☐ NO |

**Final Draft**   Now, using the self-evaluation, write your final draft.

-------------------------------------------------------------

-------------------------------------------------------------

-------------------------------------------------------------

-------------------------------------------------------------

-------------------------------------------------------------

-------------------------------------------------------------

-------------------------------------------------------------

-------------------------------------------------------------

-------------------------------------------------------------

-------------------------------------------------------------

-------------------------------------------------------------

**Evaluate Your Partner's Essay**   Read your partner's essay and make positive and negative comments on it. Use the self-evaluation form on the previous page if you need help.

**Choose the Best Essay**   Divide into groups of four and read all of the essays. Then, decide which essay is the best. Discuss why you feel that way with your group members.

Look at the following topics. Choose one of them and write a descriptive essay.

**More Topics**

- What does your classroom look like?

- Can you describe your bedroom in as much detail as possible?

- What does your favorite type of car look like?

- What does/did your high school uniform look like?

- How does your mother/father look?

# 08 Your Characteristics

**WRITING ASSIGNMENT**    What kind of a person are you? How would you describe your personality? Do you have any characteristics that make you unique?

**Building Background**    Read the following quiz. Then, answer the questions.

## | The Introvert/Extrovert Quiz |

As a general rule, introverts are quiet, private individuals while extroverts are louder and more outgoing. But there is more to being an introvert or extrovert than those characteristics. Take the following quiz by answering each question with *true* or *false*. Then, you can figure out how introverted or extroverted you are.

| | | | |
|---|---|---|---|
| 1 | At school, I prefer lectures to class discussions. | ☐ True | ☐ False |
| 2 | I enjoy spending time alone. | ☐ True | ☐ False |
| 3 | I have been told that I am a good listener. | ☐ True | ☐ False |
| 4 | I tend to avoid arguments or fights with others. | ☐ True | ☐ False |
| 5 | I do my best work alone rather than in groups. | ☐ True | ☐ False |
| 6 | It is easy for me to concentrate on various tasks. | ☐ True | ☐ False |
| 7 | I give careful consideration before I make a statement. | ☐ True | ☐ False |
| 8 | I have less interest in money, fame, and status than my friends. | ☐ True | ☐ False |
| 9 | I have little interest in multitasking. | ☐ True | ☐ False |
| 10 | I prefer to attend small gatherings with friends and family members than with people I know casually or have never met before. | ☐ True | ☐ False |
| 11 | I enjoy talking about topics in depth rather than engaging in small talk. | ☐ True | ☐ False |
| 12 | I avoid taking risks but generally do safe things. | ☐ True | ☐ False |

Now, count the number of *true* and *false* responses you gave. If you answered *true* more often, you have introverted qualities. If you responded *false* more often, you are more of an extroverted person.

1    According to the quiz, what kinds of people are most likely introverts and extroverts?

2    How did you do on the quiz? Are you more introverted or extroverted? Do you agree with the results of the quiz? Why or why not?

**Brainstorming**   Think about the topic and brainstorm some ideas for your essay. Refer to the words and definitions below for help. Then, answer the questions.

**Building Ideas**

| My Characteristics | | |
|---|---|---|
| Characteristic 1 | Characteristic 2 | Characteristic 3 |
| | | |

**Building Vocabulary**

**characteristic** (n) a trait; a feature; a quality

**personality** (n) the total sum of a person's characteristics; the collection of qualities that define a person

**describe** (v) to explain something in detail

**characterize** (v) to say that a person has some type of quality

**outgoing** (adj) friendly and sociable; talkative

**silent** (adj) quiet

**honest** (adj) fair; telling the truth

**trustworthy** (adj) able to be believed by others

**competitive** (adj) having a strong desire to win or succeed

**responsible** (adj) reliable; dependable

**irresponsible** (adj) unreliable; not dependable

**argumentative** (adj) having the tendency to disagree with others or to get into verbal fights with others

**pleasant** (adj) nice to be around; cheerful

**openminded** (adj) showing a willingness to listen to or adopt new ideas; unbiased

**narrowminded** (adj) unwilling to listen to or adopt new ideas; biased

**considerate** (adj) polite; showing a kind awareness toward other people and their problems

**brave** (adj) having courage; not afraid

**charming** (adj) having a pleasant personality

**conscientious** (adj) acting according to a sense of what is right and wrong

**determined** (adj) set in one's purpose or opinion

**stylish** (adj) elegant; acting or appearing in a manner that is considered standard by society

**creative** (adj) coming up with new ideas; imaginative

**logical** (adj) rational; using reasoning to determine one's behavior or actions

**emotional** (adj) using feelings to determine one's behavior or actions

**diligent** (adj) hardworking; constantly trying to accomplish something

*Fill in the blanks with the words above.*

1    Jason is _____ , so you can count on him to do his job properly.

2    Do you think you can _____ your personality for everyone?

*Choose the correct words for the sentences.*

3    When he becomes (emotional / logical), he sometimes yells at his employees.

4    You have a (responsible / charming) personality that makes people like you.

## Making an Outline

Look at the ideas you came up with in the brainstorming section. Then, use them to create an outline for your essay.

### Introduction

### Body

| Detail 1 | Detail 2 | Detail 3 |

### Conclusion

## First Draft

Use the outline you wrote above to write the first draft of your essay.

## Using Personal Examples

When writing an essay, it is often necessary to include examples in your body paragraphs. They can strengthen the argument you are trying to make. In many cases, you can include personal examples with stories from or information about your own life.

Personal examples are vital for essays whose topics are about you, your feelings, your likes, or similar topics. If you avoid using them, your essay will be boring, bland, and unpersuasive. By using them, you can provide a personal touch to your essay by revealing information about yourself that the reader will find interesting.

When using personal examples, make sure they are relevant to the topic. You do not need to include private or secret information which you would rather not reveal. Instead, tell stories about events that happened to you in the past. These are frequently interesting to readers and can help convince them of the point you are making.

**Model Essay**    Read the following sample essay. Underline the personal examples.

## My Characteristics

There are many words that could be used to describe my characteristics. However, if I had to choose just three, they would be friendly, hardworking, and curious.

I go out of my way to be friendly to others. I am also nice and considerate toward my friends, and I make an effort to become friends with people who look lonely. Last weekend, I saw a person at a café who looked a bit down. I went to his table and asked if I could sit with him. He agreed, and we started a conversation. By the time it ended, he looked much happier than before.

I am also a hardworking individual. It does not matter what kind of task, chore, or homework or work assignment I am doing. If I have something to do, I work hard to do it to the best of my ability. Thanks to this ability, I do good work and also complete it on time.

Finally, I consider myself a curious person. When I hear about something new, I get interested in it and try to learn more. Two weeks ago, I was watching a TV program on ancient history. It was so interesting that I became curious about that period of time, so I went to the library to learn more about it. That is just one example of how curious I can be.

Friendliness, the ability to work hard, and curiosity are three words that define me. They are some of my most important characteristics, and they have a big influence on my personality.

Compound sentences combine two sentences with each other. To do this, use a coordinating conjunction such as *and*, *but*, *or*, or *so*. Each part of a compound sentence has a subject and a verb, so you need to put a comma in front of the conjunction.

- I am honest, **and** my friends really like me.
- Are you logical, **or** are you more emotional?
- She is talkative, **but** she can also be quiet.
- David likes new ideas, **so** he is very openminded.

*Write one compound sentence each using "and," "but," "or," and "so."*

1 ........................................................................................................................................

2 ........................................................................................................................................

3 ........................................................................................................................................

4 ........................................................................................................................................

*Circle the coordinating conjunctions when they create compound sentences in the essay on the previous page.*

**Self-Evaluation**   Reread your first draft. Then, complete the following self-evaluation.

| | | | |
|---|---|---|---|
| 1 | Did I write a five-paragraph essay? | ☐ YES | ☐ NO |
| 2 | Did I include a thesis statement in the introduction? | ☐ YES | ☐ NO |
| 3 | Did I use examples in each body paragraph? | ☐ YES | ☐ NO |
| 4 | Did I include a topic statement in each body paragraph? | ☐ YES | ☐ NO |
| 5 | Did I restate the thesis statement in the conclusion? | ☐ YES | ☐ NO |
| 6 | Did I use correct grammar? | ☐ YES | ☐ NO |
| 7 | Did I use correct spelling? | ☐ YES | ☐ NO |
| 8 | Did I use correct punctuation? | ☐ YES | ☐ NO |
| 9 | Did I use sequence words properly? | ☐ YES | ☐ NO |
| 10 | Did I use transition words well? | ☐ YES | ☐ NO |
| 11 | Did I avoid using contractions? | ☐ YES | ☐ NO |
| 12 | Did I make logical arguments? | ☐ YES | ☐ NO |

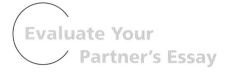

**Final Draft**  Now, using the self-evaluation, write your final draft.

**Evaluate Your Partner's Essay**  Read your partner's essay and make positive and negative comments on it. Use the self-evaluation form on the previous page if you need help.

**Choose the Best Essay**  Divide into groups of four and read all of the essays. Then, decide which essay is the best. Discuss why you feel that way with your group members.

Look at the following topics. Choose one of them and write a descriptive essay.

**More Topics**

- What are some of your best friend's characteristics?

- What three characteristics would you like to have?

- Can you describe three types of personalities?

- How can people with introverted personalities benefit?

- How can people with extroverted personalities benefit?

# 09 A Place You Would Like to Visit

**WRITING ASSIGNMENT**

Where would you like to go in the future? Why? What would you like to see there, or what activities would you like to do there?

## Building Background

Read the following travel diary. Then, answer the questions.

**June 18**

I arrived in Paris, France, and checked into my hotel. I immediately went out to visit the Eiffel Tower and the Arch of Triumph. Following that, I spent all day at the Louvre Museum. The artwork was incredible, and the other exhibits, especially the one with the Egyptian artifacts, were impressive.

**June 21**

I got to London, England, rented a car, and made a two-hour drive to see Stonehenge. I got to cross that off my bucket list. I've wanted to see Stonehenge in person ever since I was a young man. It was so awe inspiring. I'm driving north to see Hadrian's Wall next.

**June 24**

My flight from Manchester, England, arrived in Zurich, Switzerland, in the morning, so that gave me plenty of time to take a tour of the city. I love Swiss architecture and the natural scenery here.

**June 26**

I finally made it to the city of my dreams: Rome, Italy. I arrived too late at night to do any sightseeing today, so I planned my itinerary for the next few days. I'm going to be at the Vatican for the entire day tomorrow. I can't wait to visit St. Peter's Cathedral. And I'm really looking forward to seeing Michelangelo's artwork in person. The next day, I'll visit some ancient Roman ruins, including the Colosseum. The following day, I plan to visit some of the city's museums. I'll also be sure to dine at some of Rome's top restaurants because Italian food is simply the best.

1   What is the diary writer going to do in each country?

2   Which place looks the most interesting to you? Why would you like to go there?

**Brainstorming** Think about the topic and brainstorm some ideas for your essay. Refer to the words and definitions below for help. Then, answer the questions.

## Building Ideas

| A Place I Would Like to Visit | | |
| --- | --- | --- |
| Destination | Reason | Activities |
| | | |

## Building Vocabulary

**sightsee** *(v)* to travel to a place for the purpose of seeing places of interest

**abroad** *(adv)* in or to a foreign country

**booking** *(n)* a reservation

**destination** *(n)* the place where one is going

**itinerary** *(n)* a detailed travel plan

**schedule** *(v)* to plan to do something at a certain time on a certain date

**trek** *(n)* a long or difficult trip

**jungle** *(n)* a wild land with very thick vegetation

**rainforest** *(n)* a tropical forest

**ruins** *(n)* the destroyed remains of a building from the past, often one made centuries ago

**ancient** *(adj)* very old

**extinct** *(adj)* no longer in existence

**archaeology** *(n)* the study of ancient or prehistoric people and their civilizations

**scuba dive** *(v)* to use breathing equipment to swim underwater

**snorkeling** *(n)* to use a mask and a snorkel, a breathing apparatus, to be able to look underwater

**cruise** *(n)* a trip on a large ship

**cruise ship** *(n)* a large ship that carries passengers from one location to another on pleasure trips

**adventure** *(n)* an exciting, and sometimes dangerous, trip

**romantic** *(adj)* relating to love or fanciful feelings

**road trip** *(n)* a trip in which the travelers drive to their destination

**safari** *(n)* a trip done for the purpose of hunting or observing animals, often in Africa

**festival** *(n)* a periodic celebration of a special day or event

**tropics** *(n)* the part of the Earth that often gets hot, humid weather all year long

**paradise** *(n)* a peaceful place of great beauty

*Fill in the blanks with the words above.*

1    The travel agent completed the traveler's _____ and sent it to him.

2    We plan to sail to Aruba on a _____ .

*Choose the correct words for the sentences.*

3    They are going to spend some time in the (trek / tropics) for their next vacation.

4    I will go on a (safari / road trip) in Africa to see lions, zebras, and elephants.

## Making an Outline

Look at the ideas you came up with in the brainstorming section. Then, use them to create an outline for your essay.

### Introduction

### Body

| Detail 1 | Detail 2 | Detail 3 |

### Conclusion

## First Draft

Use the outline you wrote above to write the first draft of your essay.

## Avoiding Unnecessary Adverbs

Adverbs can be useful in writing, but some writers tend to overuse them. There is a time to use adverbs, and there is a time to avoid them.

Adverbs like *slowly* and *fast* can be helpful. For instance, "He walked slowly" is a good use of an adverb. But "She whispered softly" is not. The reason is that all whispering is soft, so using *softly* is repetitive and therefore unnecessary.

Adverbs like *very* and *really* are overused all the time. Instead of using expressions like *very big*, try *large* or *enormous* instead. And do not write *really funny*. Instead, use *hilarious* or *comical*. In these cases, you can replace an adverb and an adjective with a more descriptive adjective.

Finally, do not use the word *literally*. Most people use this word when they should use the word *figuratively*. *Literally* is overused and used improperly, so it would be best to avoid it.

**Model Essay**    Read the following sample essay. Underline the adverbs and decide if they are necessary or unnecessary.

# Where I Would Like to Go in the Future

I would love to visit hundreds of places around the world. However, one place that really stands out in my mind is Hawaii. If I could travel to Hawaii, it would be like a dream come true.

For starters, Hawaii has a tropical climate, so the weather is pretty hot there all year long. In my home country, the weather is very cold and snowy in winter. Last winter, there was snow on the ground for most of December and January. If I visited Hawaii in winter, I could forget about cold temperatures and simply enjoy my time there.

I am also a very huge fan of the beach, and Hawaii has plenty of beautiful beaches. I love swimming and getting a suntan on the beach. I want to try snorkeling, too. I heard it is possible to see numerous tropical fish close to shore by going snorkeling. That would be a great experience.

Lastly, Hawaii has some totally interesting geology that I am interested in exploring. There are rainforests I want to trek through. Hiking to the top of Diamond Head, a mountain near Honolulu, and seeing the sunrise would be amazing. I would also like to visit the volcanoes like Mauna Loa on one of the Hawaiian Islands. Visiting those places would literally make my trip perfect.

Hawaii stands out as one place I would love to visit in the future. It has really outstanding weather, great beaches, and unique geography. I hope to travel there one day.

> **Grammar in Writing**
>
> Use "**would + verb**" to talk about a desire, hope, or wish for the future. Use "**would not + verb**" to express the negative form.
>
> - I would like to fly around the world.
> - They would not enjoy that art gallery.
> - It would be great to travel to Easter Island.
> - It would not be fun to go camping in the jungle.

*Write two sentences with "would + verb" and two sentences with "would not + verb."*

1 _____

2 _____

3 _____

4 _____

*Circle "would + verb" in the essay on the previous page.*

## Self-Evaluation   Reread your first draft. Then, complete the following self-evaluation.

| | | | |
|---|---|---|---|
| 1 | Did I write a five-paragraph essay? | ☐ YES | ☐ NO |
| 2 | Did I include a thesis statement in the introduction? | ☐ YES | ☐ NO |
| 3 | Did I use examples in each body paragraph? | ☐ YES | ☐ NO |
| 4 | Did I include a topic statement in each body paragraph? | ☐ YES | ☐ NO |
| 5 | Did I restate the thesis statement in the conclusion? | ☐ YES | ☐ NO |
| 6 | Did I use correct grammar? | ☐ YES | ☐ NO |
| 7 | Did I use correct spelling? | ☐ YES | ☐ NO |
| 8 | Did I use correct punctuation? | ☐ YES | ☐ NO |
| 9 | Did I use sequence words properly? | ☐ YES | ☐ NO |
| 10 | Did I use transition words well? | ☐ YES | ☐ NO |
| 11 | Did I avoid using contractions? | ☐ YES | ☐ NO |
| 12 | Did I make logical arguments? | ☐ YES | ☐ NO |

**Final Draft**  Now, using the self-evaluation, write your final draft.

**Evaluate Your Partner's Essay**  Read your partner's essay and make positive and negative comments on it. Use the self-evaluation form on the previous page if you need help.

**Choose the Best Essay**  Divide into groups of four and read all of the essays. Then, decide which essay is the best. Discuss why you feel that way with your group members.

Look at the following topics. Choose one of them and write a descriptive essay.

**More Topics**

- Where did you go on your last vacation?

- What is a popular tourist destination in your country?

- Can you describe a well-known landmark in your city?

- What do you consider the ideal vacation to be?

- Where would you like to live in the future?

# 10 Your Favorite Class

**WRITING ASSIGNMENT**  Since you started attending school, what has been your favorite class? What subject was it? Why did you like that class so much?

## Building Background   Read the following magazine article. Then, answer the questions.

## Teaching Methods

*by Anna Marvin*

Not all teachers teach the same way. In fact, there are many teaching methods that instructors can use to provide their students with the knowledge they need to be successful in the future. Here are a few of them:

**1) The Lecture Style**: This style is common in classes such as history. The teacher simply talks to the students and provides them with information. Students typically take notes and are expected to memorize or remember the information the teacher lectures on.

**2) The Demonstration Style**: This style is similar to the lecture style, but the teacher demonstrates the information being taught. So a math teacher may show the students how to solve problems by solving them on the board. Other teachers using this method might employ PowerPoint presentations or show videos to their students.

**3) The Group Style**: This style requires students to work in groups. It is ideal for science classes that involve laboratory work. Other classes, such as creative writing, often require feedback from students, so teachers in those classes use this method.

**4) The Activity Style**: This style involves teachers doing various activities with students to get them to show the knowledge that they have learned. It may require students in art classes to paint or draw pictures while students in music classes may need to sing songs or play musical instruments to improve their knowledge and abilities.

1   What are four teaching methods, and which classes are they used in?

2   Which teaching method do you like the most? Which teaching method do you dislike the most?

## Brainstorming

Think about the topic and brainstorm some ideas for your essay. Refer to the words and definitions below for help. Then, answer the questions.

### Building Ideas

| My Favorite Class | | | |
| --- | --- | --- | --- |
| Class and Teacher | Reason 1 | Reason 2 | Reason 3 |
| | | | |

### Building Vocabulary

**lecture** *(v)* to teach a class by providing information to students that they are expected to remember

**discussion** *(n)* a talk about a certain topic that involves two or more people

**group activity** *(n)* a type of schoolwork that requires three or more students to work together

**project** *(n)* a special type of homework that may take several weeks to complete

**assignment** *(n)* homework; any kind of schoolwork given by a teacher to students

**submit** *(v)* to turn in something such as homework or a test

**submission** *(n)* something that a student has turned in to a teacher

**thesis** *(n)* a long research paper involving original work

**enlightening** *(adj)* informative

**captivating** *(adj)* very interesting; so interesting that a person is concentrating hard on a certain thing

**exam** *(n)* a test

**quiz** *(n)* a short test, often one that is given with no warning

**feedback** *(n)* an evaluation of a performance that contains both praise and criticism

**support** *(v)* to help a person do something

**encourage** *(v)* to inspire a person to do better or try harder

**motivate** *(v)* to provide a person with a reason to do something

**GPA** *(n)* grade point average; a way of measuring a student's overall performance at school

**graduate** *(v)* to complete a course of study at a school

**diploma** *(n)* a paper one receives that proves that one fulfilled all of the requirements at a school

**degree** *(n)* an academic title given by a college or university to a student who fulfills certain requirements

**major** *(n)* a subject a student focuses primarily upon during a course of study

**minor** *(n)* a subject a student focuses upon less than a major during a course of study

**pass** *(v)* to perform well on a test

**fail** *(v)* to perform poorly on a test

**debate** *(n)* a discussion in which two people or groups consider a question or position and take opposite sides

*Fill in the blanks with the words above.*

1   The teacher makes the students _____ their homework when class starts.

2   The doctor hangs his college _____ up in his office.

*Choose the correct words for the sentences.*

3   The teacher led a (discussion / thesis) in which the history of Rome was covered.

4   If you (pass / fail) the test, you will be able to graduate.

## Making an Outline

Look at the ideas you came up with in the brainstorming section. Then, use them to create an outline for your essay.

### Introduction

### Body

| Detail 1 | Detail 2 | Detail 3 |
|----------|----------|----------|

### Conclusion

## First Draft

Use the outline you wrote above to write the first draft of your essay.

## Varying Sentence Length

When you write an essay, it is important that you vary the length of your sentences. You want to have sentences that are both long and short.

If you do not vary your sentence length, your essay will read poorly. For instance, imagine if you wrote only short sentences. Your essay might look like this: "My favorite class was history. I took it in high school. Ms. Ellis was the teacher. I loved her class. It was so much fun." While every sentence is grammatically correct, the essay does not read well. Likewise, you do not want an essay in which every sentence has twenty or more words.

Instead, vary the sentence length. If you write a long sentence, follow it up with a short one. This can do two things: First, it can give the reader a break from the long sentence. Second, it can provide emphasis, making the short sentence important. Using this method can make your essay read better.

**Model Essay**   Read the following sample essay. Underline the short sentences.

### My Favorite Class

When I was a high school student, I was uninterested in learning. As a matter of fact, I was a poor student with terrible grades. Then, I took Mr. Lambert's math class. At that moment, everything changed. The class I took with him during my junior year of high school is my favorite class.

First of all, Mr. Lambert had a way of making the material he was teaching seem easy. I was never good at math, so I was not looking forward to his class. However, Mr. Lambert's explanations were so clear that I did well in his class. In fact, I rarely missed any problems and got A+'s on most of my tests.

Secondly, Mr. Lambert always encouraged the students to study hard and to do their best. He believed all students could do math. He stated this belief so much that everybody came to think it was true. Many students performed well in his class.

Third, Mr. Lambert did not just use class time to teach us math. He taught us other things. These included the importance of getting a good education, the need to work hard, and the need to believe in yourself. I gained a lot of confidence thanks to that class. Today, I still remember it fondly.

Mr. Lambert's math class is my favorite class of all time, and he helped me become a better student and person. To this day, I always visit him on Teacher's Day to give him a present and to thank him for helping me.

**Grammar in Writing**

**Adverbs of frequency** include *always*, *usually*, *often*, *sometimes*, *seldom*, *rarely*, and *never*. Use them to describe how often something happens. Use "**subject + adverb + verb**" or "**subject + adverb + be verb**" when you make sentences with them.

- Mr. Campbell always made class interesting.
- This class is usually entertaining.
- Her lectures often contained important information.
- Music class was never boring to me.

*Write two sentences with "subject + adverb + verb" and two sentences with "subject + adverb + be verb."*

1 _____

2 _____

3 _____

4 _____

*Circle the adverbs of frequency in the essay on the previous page.*

**Self-Evaluation**    Reread your first draft. Then, complete the following self-evaluation.

| | | | |
|---|---|---|---|
| 1 | Did I write a five-paragraph essay? | ☐ YES | ☐ NO |
| 2 | Did I include a thesis statement in the introduction? | ☐ YES | ☐ NO |
| 3 | Did I use examples in each body paragraph? | ☐ YES | ☐ NO |
| 4 | Did I include a topic statement in each body paragraph? | ☐ YES | ☐ NO |
| 5 | Did I restate the thesis statement in the conclusion? | ☐ YES | ☐ NO |
| 6 | Did I use correct grammar? | ☐ YES | ☐ NO |
| 7 | Did I use correct spelling? | ☐ YES | ☐ NO |
| 8 | Did I use correct punctuation? | ☐ YES | ☐ NO |
| 9 | Did I use sequence words properly? | ☐ YES | ☐ NO |
| 10 | Did I use transition words well? | ☐ YES | ☐ NO |
| 11 | Did I avoid using contractions? | ☐ YES | ☐ NO |
| 12 | Did I make logical arguments? | ☐ YES | ☐ NO |

## Final Draft

Now, using the self-evaluation, write your final draft.

## Evaluate Your Partner's Essay

Read your partner's essay and make positive and negative comments on it. Use the self-evaluation form on the previous page if you need help.

## Choose the Best Essay

Divide into groups of four and read all of the essays. Then, decide which essay is the best. Discuss why you feel that way with your group members.

Look at the following topics. Choose one of them and write a descriptive essay.

**More Topics**

- Who was your favorite teacher in elementary school?

- What was your middle school like?

- What was the hardest test you ever took?

- Which classroom do you remember the most, and what did it look like?

- Who was your worst teacher, and what made that teacher so bad?

# 3

# Persuasive Writing

The purpose of **persuasive writing** is to convince the reader that the writer's opinion is correct. Persuasive writing should employ rhetoric and normally appeals to emotions rather than to logic. This type of writing is found in editorials in newspapers and magazines. It is also used in political campaigns and debates.

A work of persuasive writing should have an introduction that clearly states the writer's opinion regarding the topic. Then, each body paragraph should focus on a single point. The strongest argument should come in the first body paragraph. Finally, the conclusion should restate the writer's opinion and show how it was proven correct in the body of the essay.

Here are some examples of persuasive writing.


**Example 1**

Classes at school start too early, so they should be moved back to a later time. Young people do not get enough sleep these days, so they should not be obligated to wake up at six or seven in the morning. When they go to school half-asleep, their minds and bodies are not functioning properly, which makes them unable to learn well. If schools were to start teaching classes at around eleven in the morning, students would be more alert. This would let them learn better, and they would therefore gain more knowledge over the course of the schoolyear.


**Example 2**

It is vital that humans colonize the moon and some of the planets in the solar system. If humans only remain on the Earth, a global catastrophe such as a nuclear war or an asteroid strike could cause humanity to go extinct. However, by establishing colonies throughout the solar system, we can guarantee that the human race will survive. Colonies could also serve as the stepping stones for interstellar travel to the rest of the galaxy. Humans could additionally take advantage of the minerals and other raw materials found throughout the solar system to create thriving colonies in many places.

# 11 Recycling

**WRITING ASSIGNMENT**

Do you agree or disagree with the following statement: Everyone should recycle. State your opinion. Then, defend your opinion by using facts, examples, and reasons.

**Building Background**   Read the following magazine article. Then, answer the questions.

## Renewable and Nonrenewable Resources

**Writer** *Kevin Winter*

There are numerous resources that can be found on the Earth. Despite their great numbers, they can all be placed into two categories: renewable and nonrenewable resources.

Renewable resources are those that either exist in unlimited amounts or can be replaced over the passage of time. The sun's light is a renewable resource since it will last for billions of years. This makes solar power a renewable source of energy. Hydropower, which comes from water, and geothermal power, which comes from the Earth's heat, are also renewable resources.

Trees are another renewable resource because they can grow over the course of time. The wind and the air are renewable resources, and so is biomass. This refers to the animals on the planet since they are capable of reproducing.

As for nonrenewable resources, they exist in limited amounts. Therefore, whenever the supply of them on the Earth is exhausted, they will no longer be available, or they will not be available again for a very long time. Metals such as gold, silver, copper, and iron are nonrenewable resources. The fossil fuels coal, oil, and gas are nonrenewable resources. And the fuel needed to run nuclear reactors is also a nonrenewable resource.

Regarding water, it is a renewable resource since the amount of water in all three forms on the Earth always remains constant. However, it is considered a nonrenewable resource in places affected by drought or dry weather since it may not reappear in those places after it is used.

1   What are the two types of resources? What are some examples of each type?

2   How do you think people can conserve resources? In your opinion, which methods are the best?

## Brainstorming

Think about the topic and brainstorm some ideas for your essay. Refer to the words and definitions below for help. Then, answer the questions.

### Building Ideas

| Everyone Should Recycle | | | |
| --- | --- | --- | --- |
| Opinion | Reason 1 | Reason 2 | Reason 3 |
| | | | |

### Building Vocabulary

**recycle** *(v)* to treat something so that the materials it is made of can be used again

**reduce** *(v)* to decrease the amount of something being used

**reuse** *(v)* to use something again

**plastic** *(n)* a synthetic material that is hard and can be used to make bottles and other similar objects

**container** *(n)* something into which other objects, especially solids and liquids, can be placed

**garbage** *(n)* trash; any item that is not needed and can be thrown away

**landfill** *(n)* a place where large amounts of trash are taken

**fumes** *(n)* smoke that often smells bad and is harmful

**toxic** *(adj)* poisonous; dangerous

**pollution** *(n)* anything that makes the land, water, or air dirty or unclean

**pollute** *(v)* to make the land, water, or air dirty or unclean

**compost** *(n)* a combination of rotting organic material that is often used as fertilizer

**environment** *(n)* a specific area

**habitat** *(n)* a place where a certain animal or plant can be found living

**ecosystem** *(n)* all of the organic and inorganic materials in a certain place

**degrade** *(v)* to break down, often over time

**biodegradable** *(adj)* able to be broken down due to natural causes

**organic** *(adj)* relating to living organisms

**sustainability** *(n)* able to be supported, especially for a long period of time

**renew** *(v)* to restore; to make something good again

**renewable resource** *(n)* a resource that exists in unlimited amounts

**nonrenewable resource** *(n)* a resource that exists in limited amounts

**waste** *(v)* to use something in a way that is useless or not profitable

**economize** *(v)* to be thrifty; to be efficient in one's use of something

*Fill in the blanks with the words above.*

1   Paper is _____ , so it can break down quickly.

2   Some companies _____ rivers by dumping garbage into them.

*Choose the correct words for the sentences.*

3   It is better to (reduce / reuse) those items so that you do not have to buy more of them.

4   Because those fumes are (toxic / organic), people should not breathe them.

## Making an Outline

Look at the ideas you came up with in the brainstorming section. Then, use them to create an outline for your essay.

### Introduction

### Body

| Detail 1 | Detail 2 | Detail 3 |
| --- | --- | --- |
| | | |

### Conclusion

## First Draft

Use the outline you wrote above to write the first draft of your essay.

## Stating Opinions

Sometimes you have to write an essay in which you state your opinion. There are many words and phrases you can use to do this.

One way to state your opinion in a nonacademic paper is to use phrases such as *I believe, I think, I feel,* and *I consider.* You can also use *in my opinion* and *it is my belief that.* However, in academic writing, you want to avoid using the words *I* and *my.* So phrases such as *it seems that, it could be argued that, it appears that,* and *the evidence suggests that* are better.

You can also use comparisons and contrasts to state your opinion. For instance, you might write, "While some people are uninterested in reusing products, in my opinion, doing that is extremely important," or "Although not all people recycle, I feel that everyone should."

## Model Essay

Read the following sample essay. Underline the sentences that express opinions.

### Everyone Should Recycle

I believe everyone should recycle. There are several positive results of recycling. In addition, if we do not recycle, there could be many negative effects. In my opinion, every person should recycle as much as possible.

First of all, recycling allows us to conserve our planet's natural resources. Many of the Earth's natural resources are nonrenewable ones, so there is a limited supply of them. For instance, metals, coal, oil, and gas are all nonrenewable resources. If we recycle materials that are made with them, then we can use fewer valuable resources and save them for future generations.

Another thing is that it is wasteful simply to throw away many items after using them. Landfills these days are full of plastic, glass, and metal products. Instead of throwing these items away, we should recycle them. These products can then either be reused or turned into other products that people can use.

Finally, if we do not recycle, there will be countless problems. For example, garbage dumps will become full of unrecycled products that do not break down for centuries. That will waste large amounts of land. In addition, many unrecycled items will be thrown onto the land and into the water and therefore create pollution. So not recycling would have the effect of harming the Earth.

Recycling can conserve natural resources and let us reuse them. It can also prevent the wasting of land and the creating of pollution. Because recycling has so many benefits, I think everyone should do it.

Grammar in Writing

**Gerunds** are verbs that act like nouns. Thus they serve as subjects or objects in sentences. To form a gerund, simply use the -ing form of the verb.

- **Recycling** is something everyone should do.
- **Discovering** new energy sources is important.
- John likes **reusing** the items he owns.
- We enjoy **making** new things from old ones.

***Write two sentences with a gerund as a subject and two sentences with a gerund as an object.***

1 ______________________________

2 ______________________________

3 ______________________________

4 ______________________________

***Circle the gerunds in the essay on the previous page.***

## Self-Evaluation

Reread your first draft. Then, complete the following self-evaluation.

| | | | |
|---|---|---|---|
| 1 | Did I write a five-paragraph essay? | ☐ YES | ☐ NO |
| 2 | Did I include a thesis statement in the introduction? | ☐ YES | ☐ NO |
| 3 | Did I use examples in each body paragraph? | ☐ YES | ☐ NO |
| 4 | Did I include a topic statement in each body paragraph? | ☐ YES | ☐ NO |
| 5 | Did I restate the thesis statement in the conclusion? | ☐ YES | ☐ NO |
| 6 | Did I use correct grammar? | ☐ YES | ☐ NO |
| 7 | Did I use correct spelling? | ☐ YES | ☐ NO |
| 8 | Did I use correct punctuation? | ☐ YES | ☐ NO |
| 9 | Did I use sequence words properly? | ☐ YES | ☐ NO |
| 10 | Did I use transition words well? | ☐ YES | ☐ NO |
| 11 | Did I avoid using contractions? | ☐ YES | ☐ NO |
| 12 | Did I make logical arguments? | ☐ YES | ☐ NO |

**Final Draft**  Now, using the self-evaluation, write your final draft.

**Evaluate Your Partner's Essay**  Read your partner's essay and make positive and negative comments on it. Use the self-evaluation form on the previous page if you need help.

**Choose the Best Essay**  Divide into groups of four and read all of the essays. Then, decide which essay is the best. Discuss why you feel that way with your group members.

Look at the following statements. Choose one of them, decide if you agree or disagree with the statement, and then write a persuasive essay.

**More Topics**

- We need to use fewer resources.
- Pollution is a big problem these days.
- Stores should not give plastic bags to their customers.
- We have to mine the moon or asteroids to obtain valuable natural resources.
- By discovering new energy sources, we can save existing natural resources on the Earth.

# 12 Voting

**WRITING ASSIGNMENT**

Do you agree or disagree with the following statement: The voting age should be lowered to 16. State your opinion. Then, defend your opinion by using facts, examples, and reasons.

## Building Background

Read the following webpage article. Then, answer the questions.

https://www.voteorelse.com

### Vote… Or Else!

**Writer** *Russell Jones*

Most of the world's countries have elections. On Election Day, eligible citizens head to a polling place and cast a ballot to vote for people running for office. In most countries, only individuals who want to vote participate in elections. This often results in about half of eligible individuals actually voting. However, in around twenty-five countries, voting is obligatory.

Having to vote if one is eligible is compulsory voting. Greece, Singapore, and many countries in South America require eligible citizens to vote. Those who fail to vote may have to pay a fine or be prosecuted by the government.

Why do these countries require their citizens to vote? For the most part, the belief is that the more people who take part in an election, the more the government actually represents the will of the people. Governments additionally claim that it makes people more interested in the political process. Since they have to vote, people will educate themselves on the candidates, their political beliefs, and their platforms.

On the other hand, some individuals comment that not voting is a political statement. They argue that those individuals who refuse to vote are showing their dislike of their governments and should be able to stay home.

Whatever the case may be, compulsory voting is here to stay. In fact, other countries are considering requiring voting, so the number of nations with compulsory voting may increase in the years to come.

1   Which countries have compulsory voting? Why do they make their citizens vote?

2   What is your opinion of compulsory voting? Do you believe everyone eligible should be forced to vote?

**Brainstorming** Think about the topic and brainstorm some ideas for your essay. Refer to the words and definitions below for help. Then, answer the questions.

## Building Ideas

| Lowering the Voting Age | | | |
| --- | --- | --- | --- |
| Opinion | Reason 1 | Reason 2 | Reason 3 |
| | | | |

## Building Vocabulary

**vote** *(v)* to select a person running for office

**voting age** *(n)* the age when a person is eligible to vote

**election** *(n)* an event where people cast votes for an individual or individuals running for office

**elect** *(v)* to choose a person for office through an election

**ballot** *(n)* a paper listing everyone running for office and on which people then make marks to select their choices

**candidate** *(n)* a person running for office

**term** *(n)* the amount of time a person elected to an office gets to serve

**mayor** *(n)* the elected leader of a city

**governor** *(n)* the elected leader of a state or province

**president** *(n)* the elected leader of a country

**represent** *(v)* to stand in place for or act as a proxy for an individual

**representative** *(n)* a person who acts for another or who acts as a proxy

**democracy** *(n)* government by the people; government in which the people have power through voting

**republic** *(n)* a type of government in which people select representatives to stand for them with regard to political matters

**politics** *(n)* the practice of running a government

**politician** *(n)* a person who is involved in the running of a government

**bill** *(n)* a draft of a proposed statute that must be voted on

**act** *(n)* a formal decision by a government or ruler

**law** *(n)* a bill that has been voted on successfully and become legal policy of a government

**corrupt** *(adj)* guilty of behaving dishonestly or of engaging in illegal behavior

**taxation** *(n)* the act of taxing the people to raise revenues for a government

**constitution** *(n)* a formal paper stating the rights and obligations of the people and a government

**debate** *(v)* to engage in a discussion in which two people or teams argue different sides

**rhetoric** *(n)* oratory; the art of making persuasive speeches

*Fill in the blanks with the words above.*

1   The politician is skilled at _____, so many people love his speeches.

2   There are several _____ running for mayor of the city.

*Choose the correct words for the sentences.*

3   Each state's senators are supposed to (represent / vote) the will of the state's residents.

4   Choose one of the names on the (bill / ballot) to vote for that person for president.

## Making an Outline

Look at the ideas you came up with in the brainstorming section. Then, use them to create an outline for your essay.

### Introduction

### Body

| Detail 1 | Detail 2 | Detail 3 |

### Conclusion

## First Draft

Use the outline you wrote above to write the first draft of your essay.

## Statistics

When writing a persuasive essay, you need to state your opinion regarding the topic. Then, you need to defend your opinion with facts. Statistics are an excellent way to provide facts.

Using statistics allows you to provide solid evidence for the argument you are making. For instance, compare the two following sentences: 1) More than half of eligible Americans voted in 2016. 2) Voter turnout in the United States election in 2016 was around fifty-eight percent. The second sentence is more powerful because it contains a solid number and is not a vague statement such as "more than half."

When using statistics, be careful not to overuse them. Too many numbers can be overwhelming to readers. In addition, make sure the statistics you provide are relevant to your argument. Finally, present the numbers clearly and in a way that readers can understand.

## Model Essay
Read the following sample essay. Underline the statistics.

### Lower the Voting Age

In my country, the voting age is eighteen, but that is too high. Instead, the voting age should be lowered to sixteen for a number of important reasons.

Sixteen-year-olds already act like adults in many ways, so we should treat them like adults by letting them vote. For instance, in my country, around thirty percent of sixteen-year-olds have jobs, which is adult behavior. They are taking part in the economy and paying taxes, so they should get to vote. Three of my teenage cousins have jobs. It is not fair that they cannot vote.

In addition, adults often complain that teenagers are not interested in politics or the political process. But only about sixty-five percent of eligible voters participated in the last election. Teens usually do not care about politics since they cannot vote, and that feeling extends to adulthood. But if teens were allowed to vote, many would get interested in politics. Then, the overall voter participation rate would increase.

Finally, we should not disregard the opinions of young people by preventing them from voting. A recent survey showed that seventy percent of teenagers hesitated to state their opinions because they felt that adults would ignore them. If the voting age were decreased, adults would have to listen to teens and their ideas.

It is imperative that the voting age be lowered to sixteen. Sixteen-year-olds work and pay taxes like adults. And voting will make them more interested in politics and obligate adults to listen to them and their opinions.

| | |
|---|---|
| **Grammar in Writing** | Use the **subjunctive mood** to express wishes and hypothetical situations. You can also use it when making suggestion and demands. To use the subjunctive mood, use *be* or *were* in place of *am, is, are,* or *was.* Any verbs following the *be* verb should be in the past participle form. In addition, do not use third-person -s, -es, or -ies endings. |

- If I **were** the president, I would become famous.
- It is important that they **be informed** of the problem.
- I suggest that she **be elected** mayor of the city.
- We recommend that he **receive** punishment.

*Write two sentences in the subjunctive mood with "be" or "were" and two sentences in the subjunctive mood without a third person -s, -es, or -ies ending.*

1 _____

2 _____

3 _____

4 _____

*Circle the uses of the subjunctive mood in the essay on the previous page.*

## Self-Evaluation   Reread your first draft. Then, complete the following self-evaluation.

| | | | |
|---|---|---|---|
| 1 | Did I write a five-paragraph essay? | ☐ YES | ☐ NO |
| 2 | Did I include a thesis statement in the introduction? | ☐ YES | ☐ NO |
| 3 | Did I use examples in each body paragraph? | ☐ YES | ☐ NO |
| 4 | Did I include a topic statement in each body paragraph? | ☐ YES | ☐ NO |
| 5 | Did I restate the thesis statement in the conclusion? | ☐ YES | ☐ NO |
| 6 | Did I use correct grammar? | ☐ YES | ☐ NO |
| 7 | Did I use correct spelling? | ☐ YES | ☐ NO |
| 8 | Did I use correct punctuation? | ☐ YES | ☐ NO |
| 9 | Did I use sequence words properly? | ☐ YES | ☐ NO |
| 10 | Did I use transition words well? | ☐ YES | ☐ NO |
| 11 | Did I avoid using contractions? | ☐ YES | ☐ NO |
| 12 | Did I make logical arguments? | ☐ YES | ☐ NO |

**Final Draft**    Now, using the self-evaluation, write your final draft.

**Evaluate Your Partner's Essay**    Read your partner's essay and make positive and negative comments on it. Use the self-evaluation form on the previous page if you need help.

**Choose the Best Essay**    Divide into groups of four and read all of the essays. Then, decide which essay is the best. Discuss why you feel that way with your group members.

Look at the following statements. Choose one of them, decide if you agree or disagree with the statement, and then write a persuasive essay.

**More Topics**

- Foreigners living in other countries should be allowed to vote in those countries' elections.
- People who have been in prison should not be allowed to vote.
- Everyone who is eligible should be obligated to vote.
- All voting should be done by secret ballot.
- Citizens should be allowed to vote politicians out of office before their terms are over.

# 13 Pets

**WRITING ASSIGNMENT**

Do you agree or disagree with the following statement: Dogs are the best pets. State your opinion. Then, defend your opinion by using facts, examples, and reasons.

## Building Background

Read the following advertisement. Then, answer the questions.

### Petland is having a BIG SALE this weekend

Come to Petland, where we sell all kinds of pets. We have dogs, cats, hamsters, guinea pigs, parrots, fish, iguanas, turtles, and even snakes.

What's the right pet for you? Let us tell you about some of the animals we have:

**Dogs** | Do you like walking in the park? How about an active dog like a Siberian huskie, golden retriever, or dalmatian? Want to stay at home and watch TV with a lapdog? Then a shi-tzu, Yorkshire terrier, or Maltese would be perfect. Or perhaps you want a dog to protect your children? Then you should get a boxer, Saint Bernard, or German shepherd.

**Cats** | They aren't as playful or obedient as dogs, but we've got all kinds of cat breeds for sale.

Check out our Siamese, Manx, Burmese, Korat, and Bombay cats.

**Birds** | Do you desire an intelligent bird that will live for decades? Get a beautiful parrot. We also have parakeets, finches, and cockatiels.

**Rodents** | Hamsters and gerbils are great starter pets for children. Or get a guinea pig if you want a pet that's bigger but still docile.

**Fish** | These are the easiest pets to keep. Just take care of their tank and feed them daily.

**Reptiles** | Go for a more exotic pet like a python, iguana, or turtle. They're low maintenance and won't care if you're at work all day long.

1  What does the advertisement point out about each type of pet?

2  Which pet looks the most appealing to you? Why do you feel that way?

**Brainstorming** — Think about the topic and brainstorm some ideas for your essay. Refer to the words and definitions below for help. Then, answer the questions.

## Building Ideas

| Dogs Are the Best Pets | | | |
|---|---|---|---|
| Opinion | Reason 1 | Reason 2 | Reason 3 |
| | | | |

## Building Vocabulary

**pet** *(n)* an animal like a dog, cat, or hamster that a person takes care of, often in that person's home

**pet** *(v)* to move one's hand across an animal's body in a gentle and often affectionate way

**raise** *(v)* to take care of an animal by feeding it, by giving it a home, and generally by looking after it

**feed** *(v)* to give food to an animal

**groom** *(v)* to brush an animal and to look after its fur

**bathe** *(v)* to give a bath to an animal

**take for a walk** *(v)* to take an animal outside and to go walking with it

**train** *(v)* to teach an animal proper behavior

**trick** *(n)* a clever or skillful feat, such as shaking hands or rolling over, taught to an animal

**veterinarian** *(n)* an animal doctor

**checkup** *(n)* a medical health examination

**vaccine** *(n)* a medicine that provides immunity to a virus

**vaccinate** *(v)* to give a vaccine to

**adopt** *(v)* to take an animal into one's home as a pet

**rescue animal** *(n)* an animal that has been saved from a bad situation such as an abusive owner

**collar** *(n)* a band or chain that is fastened around the neck of an animal to restrain or identify it

**leash** *(n)* a chain or strap attached to an animal to control or restrain it

**flea** *(n)* a tiny insect that bites animals and may cause itching

**treat** *(n)* a snack that is often given to an animal after it behaves properly

**protect** *(v)* to keep safe

**loyal** *(adj)* faithful to a person

**unconditional love** *(n)* the act of loving someone without requirements or conditions

**bark** *(n)* the loud sound a dog makes

**cage** *(n)* a small container, often with bars, in which an animal may be kept

**kennel** *(n)* a house or shelter for animals such as dogs and cats

*Fill in the blanks with the words above.*

1  My family is planning to _____ a rescue cat next week.
2  The _____ gave my dog a checkup and said she looks fine.

*Choose the correct words for the sentences.*

3  I always give my dog a (trick / treat) when he does something good.
4  Many pets are (loyal / collar) to their owners.

## Making an Outline

Look at the ideas you came up with in the brainstorming section. Then, use them to create an outline for your essay.

### Introduction

### Body

| Detail 1 | Detail 2 | Detail 3 |

### Conclusion

## First Draft

Use the outline you wrote above to write the first draft of your essay.

## Comparing and Contrasting

Making comparisons and contrasts is a great way to convince your readers of your point when writing a persuasive essay. There are a couple of ways to make comparisons and contrasts.

The easiest way is to use comparative adjectives or the word *more* in front of an adjective. For instance, you can write, "Dogs are smarter than turtles," or "Cats are more entertaining than birds." Be sure that these comparisons and contrasts are easy to understand.

You can also make comparisons and contrasts by using expressions such as *in comparison, in contrast, on the other hand, in opposition,* and *however*.

Try to avoid using adverbs such as *very, much,* and *really* when comparing and contrasting. You want to be as specific as possible, and those words are too vague.

**Model Essay**   Read the following sample essay. Underline the comparisons and contrasts.

### Dogs: The Best Pets

People keep numerous animals as pets, including dogs, cats, birds, fish, hamsters, and reptiles. Of all these animals, dogs are by far the best pets.

For one thing, dogs are incredibly loving animals. My family has a dog that is always happy to see us. When anyone in my family goes home, Rusty is at the door to greet us. Rusty also loves spending time with us and is a great pet. In contrast, we have a cat, too. Natasha spends time by herself and does not seem to care much about us.

In addition, you can do activities with dogs that you cannot do with other pets. Every day, I take Rusty out to the park to go for a walk. I throw a stick, and he fetches it. You cannot take a hamster, fish, or a snake out for a walk. Birds and cats do not fetch either. Those animals have fewer abilities than dogs do.

Yet another thing is that dogs have been known to save their owners' lives. I have read many stories about dogs that notify people assistance is needed when their owners suffer medical problems. Recently, there was a news story about a dog that rescued a baby from a fire. A pet cat would never do anything like that.

When it comes to pets, dogs are the best animals. They are loyal, you can do fun activities with them, and they just might save your life. Clearly, people should choose dogs when selecting new pets.

The **relative pronoun *that*** can be used to refer to people, animals, and things. It can only be used in defining clauses, and it can be the subject or object of a relative clause.

- The animal that I like the most is the dolphin.
- Everyone that we invited came to the party.
- Some people have dogs that protect their homes.
- The problem that occurred was eventually solved.

*Write two sentences with "that" as the subject of a relative clause and two sentences with "that" as the object of a relative clause.*

1 ........................................................................................................

2 ........................................................................................................

3 ........................................................................................................

4 ........................................................................................................

*Circle the uses of the relative pronoun "that" in the essay on the previous page.*

**Self-Evaluation**  Reread your first draft. Then, complete the following self-evaluation.

| | | | |
|---|---|---|---|
| 1 | Did I write a five-paragraph essay? | ☐ YES | ☐ NO |
| 2 | Did I include a thesis statement in the introduction? | ☐ YES | ☐ NO |
| 3 | Did I use examples in each body paragraph? | ☐ YES | ☐ NO |
| 4 | Did I include a topic statement in each body paragraph? | ☐ YES | ☐ NO |
| 5 | Did I restate the thesis statement in the conclusion? | ☐ YES | ☐ NO |
| 6 | Did I use correct grammar? | ☐ YES | ☐ NO |
| 7 | Did I use correct spelling? | ☐ YES | ☐ NO |
| 8 | Did I use correct punctuation? | ☐ YES | ☐ NO |
| 9 | Did I use sequence words properly? | ☐ YES | ☐ NO |
| 10 | Did I use transition words well? | ☐ YES | ☐ NO |
| 11 | Did I avoid using contractions? | ☐ YES | ☐ NO |
| 12 | Did I make logical arguments? | ☐ YES | ☐ NO |

**Final Draft**   Now, using the self-evaluation, write your final draft.

**Evaluate Your Partner's Essay**   Read your partner's essay and make positive and negative comments on it. Use the self-evaluation form on the previous page if you need help.

**Choose the Best Essay**   Divide into groups of four and read all of the essays. Then, decide which essay is the best. Discuss why you feel that way with your group members.

Look at the following statements. Choose one of them, decide if you agree or disagree with the statement, and then write a persuasive essay.

**More Topics**

- Everyone should own at least one pet.

- People need to spend some time on farms to be used to living with animals.

- It should be illegal for people to own exotic animals such as lions, elephants, and zebras.

- Some dog breeds, such as pit bulls, are too dangerous to be pets.

- People who treat their pets poorly should get in trouble with the law.

# 14 Chores

**WRITING ASSIGNMENT**

Do you agree or disagree with the following statement: All children should do chores. State your opinion. Then, defend your opinion by using facts, examples, and reasons.

**Building Background**  Read the following diary entries. Then, answer the questions.

**Monday, October 1**

Woke up and made my bed. Returned home from school and walked the dog. Gave the dog a bath as well. Assisted Mom with cooking dinner and then cleaned the dishes off the table after dinner.

**Tuesday, October 2**

Didn't have enough time to make my bed in the morning so did that after school. Set the table and cleaned it off after dinner. Folded the laundry and took out the garbage.

**Wednesday, October 3**

Made my bed and cooked breakfast in the morning. Bought some groceries at the market before coming home from school. Washed the vegetables and then chopped them up. Cleaned the bathroom and scrubbed the bathtub.

**Thursday, October 4**

Was busy studying for exams on Friday so didn't do any chores at all. Parents understood.

**Friday, October 5**

Vacuumed the living room and swept the kitchen floor. Cleaned out the cat's litter box. Went to bed early so didn't do anything else.

**Saturday, October 6**

Spent two hours cleaning my room in the morning. Dusted the bookshelves in the living room and rearranged some of the furniture with Dad. Washed the dishes after dinner and did the laundry.

**Sunday, October 7**

Went to Grandma and Grandpa's house so didn't do any chores. Got back too late at night to do anything.

1   What chores did the writer do during the week?

2   Which chores do you enjoy doing? Which ones do you dislike doing? Why do you feel that way?

**Brainstorming** Think about the topic and brainstorm some ideas for your essay. Refer to the words and definitions below for help. Then, answer the questions.

## Building Ideas

| All Children Should Do Chores | | | |
| --- | --- | --- | --- |
| Opinion | Reason 1 | Reason 2 | Reason 3 |
| | | | |

## Building Vocabulary

**chore** *(n)* work often done in a house and which needs to be done daily or weekly

**make one's bed** *(phr)* to straighten the sheets on one's bed after getting up

**take out** *(v)* to remove

**garbage** *(n)* trash; anything that is not needed and can be thrown away

**set the table** *(phr)* to put dishes and utensils on a table before a meal

**clean off the table** *(phr)* to remove the dishes, utensils, and food from a table after a meal

**do the dishes** *(phr)* to wash dirty dishes and utensils

**rinse** *(v)* to remove soap from something by cleaning it with water

**dry** *(v)* to remove the water or dampness from something

**do the laundry** *(phr)* to wash one's clothes

**fold** *(v)* to bend and lay parts of something such as clothes together to make them more compact

**iron** *(v)* to use a tool to remove the wrinkles and creases from one's clothes

**take care of** *(v)* to look after

**babysit** *(v)* to watch a baby or child while the parents are away for a while

**vacuum** *(v)* to use a machine to clean a floor

**sweep** *(v)* to use a broom to clean a floor

**mop** *(v)* to use a stick with a sponge at the end of it to get a floor wet and to clean it

**allowance** *(n)* spending money that parents give a child on a weekly basis

**obligation** *(n)* something that must be done

**daily** *(adv)* every day

**punishment** *(n)* a penalty that is inflicted on a person for bad behavior

**chastise** *(v)* to criticize a person

**praise** *(v)* to say good things to or about a person

**burden** *(n)* something that makes a person's life hard or difficult

*Fill in the blanks with the words above.*

1   My parents always _____ me when I fail to do my chores.

2   Please take out the _____ because it is starting to smell bad.

*Choose the correct words for the sentences.*

3   My parents want me to (vacuum / babysit) my little brother while they go out to dinner.

4   Doing chores daily can be a big (allowance / burden) at times.

## Making an Outline

Look at the ideas you came up with in the brainstorming section. Then, use them to create an outline for your essay.

### Introduction

### Body

| Detail 1 | Detail 2 | Detail 3 |
| --- | --- | --- |

### Conclusion

## First Draft

Use the outline you wrote above to write the first draft of your essay.

## Hyperbole

A hyperbole is an extreme exaggeration. You can use hyperbole when you want to emphasize a point or to create a strong effect or feeling on the readers.

There are many examples of hyperbole. For instance, if you are hungry, you can write, "I'm so hungry that I could eat a horse." Of course, you cannot eat that much, but you are pointing out that you are very hungry. About a difficult test, you might write, "That test nearly killed me," even though you are still in good health. And about a loyal friend, you could write, "He would give me the shirt off his back," even though he did not give his shirt to you.

Hyperboles are effective at making strong impressions on readers. However, try to avoid using them too much. If you are constantly exaggerating, readers will not take your writing very seriously.

**Model Essay**    Read the following sample essay. Underline the examples of hyperbole.

## Children Should Not Do Chores

When I was a child, my parents made me do chores. I felt like I was going to die because they kept me from doing other activities. I therefore strongly oppose making children do chores.

For one thing, children need to enjoy their lives. When they are young, they ought to be outdoors playing with their friends or doing other fun activities. They do not need to be tortured by having to clean their rooms, set the table, or do the laundry. They can do those chores later when they are teenagers.

For another thing, the children in my country are already busy because of school. When I was an elementary school student, I had tons of homework. I also attended some private academies. I arrived home around eight at night, and then my parents had me do chores. I was so tired that I could barely move, so that was unfair to me.

As a final note, children are too young to do chores well, so they will not do a satisfactory job. One of my chores was washing the dishes. I tried hard, but I was the worst dishwasher in the world. My mother was always disappointed, but there was nothing I could do. I was too young to be washing the dishes.

There is no reason to have children do chores. They need to have fun and are already busy because of school, and they will not do well anyway. For those reasons, parents should not make children do chores.

**Grammar in Writing**

*Make* and *have* are both causative verbs because they cause something to happen. Use "**make + person + verb**" to force a person to do something. Use "**have + person + verb**" to give something the responsibility to do something.

- Mr. Jones **made me turn** in my homework.

- Lisa's parents **make her study** every night.

- I **had my brother clean** the bedroom.

- The teacher **has the students solve** problems in class.

*Write two sentences with "make + person + verb" and two sentences with "have + person + verb."*

1 ........................................................................................................

2 ........................................................................................................

3 ........................................................................................................

4 ........................................................................................................

*Circle the causative verbs in the essay on the previous page.*

**Self-Evaluation**  Reread your first draft. Then, complete the following self-evaluation.

| | | | |
|---|---|---|---|
| 1 | Did I write a five-paragraph essay? | ☐ YES | ☐ NO |
| 2 | Did I include a thesis statement in the introduction? | ☐ YES | ☐ NO |
| 3 | Did I use examples in each body paragraph? | ☐ YES | ☐ NO |
| 4 | Did I include a topic statement in each body paragraph? | ☐ YES | ☐ NO |
| 5 | Did I restate the thesis statement in the conclusion? | ☐ YES | ☐ NO |
| 6 | Did I use correct grammar? | ☐ YES | ☐ NO |
| 7 | Did I use correct spelling? | ☐ YES | ☐ NO |
| 8 | Did I use correct punctuation? | ☐ YES | ☐ NO |
| 9 | Did I use sequence words properly? | ☐ YES | ☐ NO |
| 10 | Did I use transition words well? | ☐ YES | ☐ NO |
| 11 | Did I avoid using contractions? | ☐ YES | ☐ NO |
| 12 | Did I make logical arguments? | ☐ YES | ☐ NO |

**Final Draft** Now, using the self-evaluation, write your final draft.

**Evaluate Your Partner's Essay** Read your partner's essay and make positive and negative comments on it. Use the self-evaluation form on the previous page if you need help.

**Choose the Best Essay** Divide into groups of four and read all of the essays. Then, decide which essay is the best. Discuss why you feel that way with your group members.

Look at the following statements. Choose one of them, decide if you agree or disagree with the statement, and then write a persuasive essay.

**More Topics**

- Parents should pay their children for doing chores.

- Children should do a variety of chores to learn life skills for the future.

- Making children do chores is child abuse.

- Homework is much more important for children than chores.

- Older children should teach their younger siblings how to do chores.

# 15 Video Games

**WRITING ASSIGNMENT**

Do you agree or disagree with the following statement: Video games are harmful. State your opinion. Then, defend your opinion by using facts, examples, and reasons.

**Building Background**   Read the following timeline. Then, answer the questions.

## A Short Timeline of Video Games

| | |
|---|---|
| **1972** | The Magnavox Odyssey, the world's first video game console, becomes available for sale. Pong, the world's first commercially successful video game, is developed. |
| **1977** | The Atari 2600 game console, the most successful console of its time, is released. |
| **1978-81** | World-famous games Asteroids, Space Invaders, and Donkey Kong are released. |
| **1985** | Nintendo releases the NES, the Nintendo Entertainment System, in the United States, as well as the game Mario Brothers, which sells ten million copies in a single year. |
| **1989** | Nintendo releases the Game Boy, which makes the game Tetris one of the most popular in history. |
| **1991** | Sega sells the Sega VR glasses, virtual reality glasses for use with its game consoles. |
| **1994** | Sony starts selling the PlayStation game console. |
| **1999** | Konami releases Dance Dance Revolution, an interactive dancing arcade game. |
| **2001** | Microsoft releases the XBOX as sixth-generation video games become popular. |
| **2003** | Mobile games become available on cellphones in Japan. |
| **2004** | Nintendo introduces a touchscreen and a stylus for its video games. |
| **2016** | Virtual reality goes mainstream thanks to the release of the Oculus Rift, the Sony PlayStation VR, and the HTC Vive, all of which are game consoles. |
| **2017** | Nintendo releases the Nintendo Switch, a console with a portable screen that lets gamers carry their game with them. |

1   What game consoles were released? When did they come out?

2   Which games listed on the timeline have you played? What did you think about those games?

**Brainstorming** Think about the topic and brainstorm some ideas for your essay. Refer to the words and definitions below for help. Then, answer the questions.

## Building Ideas

| Video Games Are Harmful | | | |
|---|---|---|---|
| Opinion | Reason 1 | Reason 2 | Reason 3 |
| | | | |

## Building Vocabulary

**game console** *(n)* a computer system that can play video games when it is hooked up to a television or computer or which can play games on a built-in screen

**joystick** *(n)* a controller for a video game

**virtual reality** *(n)* a highly realistic three-dimensional computer simulation in which a person can appear to move in a reality that is created

**resemble** *(v)* to look like; to be similar to

**realistic** *(adj)* lifelike

**practice** *(v)* to try or do something again and again to get better at it

**improve** *(v)* to get better at something

**coordination** *(n)* the act of having one's body parts move smoothly or in harmony

**teamwork** *(n)* the ability to work well with others

**winner** *(n)* a person who is victorious in a game; a person who comes in first in a game

**loser** *(n)* a person who does not come in first in a game

**strategy game** *(n)* a game which involves using plans and tactics to win

**role-playing game** *(n)* a game which involves pretending to be another person or character when playing

**shooting game** *(n)* a game which involves firing weapons

**driving game** *(n)* a game which involves manning vehicles

**aim** *(v)* to point a weapon at a target

**shoot** *(v)* to pull the trigger on a weapon to make it fire

**focus** *(v)* to pay very close attention to something

**concentration** *(n)* the act of paying close attention to something

**determination** *(n)* a feeling that one will get what one wants no matter what

**time waster** *(n)* something that is not an efficient or effective use of a person's time

**antisocial** *(adj)* unfriendly; not wanting to spend time with others

**friendless** *(adj)* having no friends or individuals one is close to

**reset** *(v)* to start a game over again

*Fill in the blanks with the words above.*

1   You need to use the _____ to control your character in the game.
2   Some games require lots of _____ so that you do not lose your focus.

*Choose the correct words for the sentences.*

3   Virtual reality games are becoming more and more (realistic / friendless) these days.
4   Be sure to (aim / shoot) the gun before you fire it at the monsters.

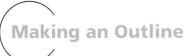

## Making an Outline

Look at the ideas you came up with in the brainstorming section. Then, use them to create an outline for your essay.

### Introduction

### Body

| Detail 1 | Detail 2 | Detail 3 |

### Conclusion

## First Draft

Use the outline you wrote above to write the first draft of your essay.

## Flow

An essay must flow well in order for it to keep the reader's attention. Flow refers to how well the sentences and paragraphs go with one another.

An excellent way to ensure that sentences and paragraphs flow well is to link them. Connect the end of one sentence with the beginning of another. This creates a natural flow so that the essay is about the same topic. For instance, if one sentence ends with a noun, start the next with a pronoun that refers to the noun in the previous sentence.

You can make sure your paragraphs flow by using transition words and sequence words. Using words such as *first, next, then, one point,* and *another point* is a way to ensure that the essay flows well. This helps the reader realize when you have finished writing about one topic and are ready to begin discussing a new one.

Read the following sample essay. Underline the words and expressions that help the essay flow well.

### The Need to Play Video Games

I do not believe that video games are harmful. In fact, I believe that they provide a number of positive benefits, so I would encourage people to play video games as much as they can.

The first reason is an obvious one: Video games are highly entertaining. I play all kinds of games with my friends, but I especially like shooting games and role-playing games. I have gotten hundreds of hours of entertainment by playing some of these games. If you want something fun to do, video games are an inexpensive and safe activity to do.

The second reason is that video games can help you improve various skills. When I play shooting games, my hand-eye coordination improves. I have to notice all of the bad guys on the screen, aim the weapons, and shoot them. When I play with my friends, I learn about teamwork. By working as a team, we can do well and win the games.

The third reason is that when you play multiplayer online games, you can meet people from around the world. During these games, I sometimes talk to the other players. I have even become friends with some of them. These people live in countries around the world, so by playing video games, I have made some foreign friends.

I strongly urge everyone to play video games. They are fun and can help you improve various skills. And it is even possible to make friends while playing them.

To describe how to do something, you can use "**by + gerund**." A gerund is the -ing form of a verb. This clause can appear anywhere in a sentence. If it starts a sentence, be sure to use a comma at the end of the clause.

- By practicing, his video game skills improved.
- He learns to play games by asking his friends for help.
- By getting a job, she managed to save money.
- They go to work by taking the subway.

*Write two sentences with "by + gerund" at the beginning of a sentence and two sentences with "by + gerund" at the end of a sentence.*

1 

2 

3 

4 

*Circle every "by + gerund" in the essay on the previous page.*

## Self-Evaluation

Reread your first draft. Then, complete the following self-evaluation.

| | | | |
|---|---|---|---|
| 1 | Did I write a five-paragraph essay? | ☐ YES | ☐ NO |
| 2 | Did I include a thesis statement in the introduction? | ☐ YES | ☐ NO |
| 3 | Did I use examples in each body paragraph? | ☐ YES | ☐ NO |
| 4 | Did I include a topic statement in each body paragraph? | ☐ YES | ☐ NO |
| 5 | Did I restate the thesis statement in the conclusion? | ☐ YES | ☐ NO |
| 6 | Did I use correct grammar? | ☐ YES | ☐ NO |
| 7 | Did I use correct spelling? | ☐ YES | ☐ NO |
| 8 | Did I use correct punctuation? | ☐ YES | ☐ NO |
| 9 | Did I use sequence words properly? | ☐ YES | ☐ NO |
| 10 | Did I use transition words well? | ☐ YES | ☐ NO |
| 11 | Did I avoid using contractions? | ☐ YES | ☐ NO |
| 12 | Did I make logical arguments? | ☐ YES | ☐ NO |

**Final Draft**   Now, using the self-evaluation, write your final draft.

**Evaluate Your Partner's Essay**   Read your partner's essay and make positive and negative comments on it. Use the self-evaluation form on the previous page if you need help.

**Choose the Best Essay**   Divide into groups of four and read all of the essays. Then, decide which essay is the best. Discuss why you feel that way with your group members.

**More Topics**

Look at the following statements. Choose one of them, decide if you agree or disagree with the statement, and then write a persuasive essay.

- Playing too many video games makes students' grades lower.

- Violent video games should be banned.

- Parents should closely monitor the video games their children play.

- Video games can teach young people many important skills.

- Being a professional gamer is a good occupation for people.

# 4

# Narrative Writing

The purpose of **narrative writing** is to tell a story. It can be autobiographical in nature and focus on the writer of the essay, or it can be biographical and be about another person or people. Narrative writing should focus on the story, so it needs to include information about the setting and the characters. This type of writing is found in storybooks and biographies. Short stories and novels contain narrative writing, and newspapers and journals may utilize it as well.

A work of narrative writing needs an introduction which describes the background, the setting, and the characters. The body paragraphs should focus on the main events in the story. And the conclusion should sum up the events and also describe any lessons that were learned through the course of the events.

Here are some examples of narrative writing.

### Example 1
I remember the first day of elementary school clearly. My mother insisted on walking into the school with me. I was embarrassed at first, but then I realized that almost every other student was being accompanied by a parent as well. When the school bell rang, I sat down in my chair. I had no idea what I was supposed to do, so I just listened carefully to my homeroom teacher and did exactly what she told the class to do. By the end of the day, I was exhausted but pleased that I had enjoyed school.

### Example 2
One night, I stayed out with my friends until late at night. I took the bus home and then started walking toward my house. While walking, I heard footsteps behind me. I turned and looked back, and then I saw a man rapidly walking toward me. I was so frightened that I did not know what to do. I started walking faster and faster, and so did the person behind me. Suddenly, as I was about to scream in terror, I heard, "Hey, Tina. Slow down." It was my friend Dave, who lived in the same apartment building as me.

# 16 A Story from Your Country's History

**WRITING ASSIGNMENT** What is an impressive story from your country's history? What happens in the story? What do you think of that story?

## Building Background

Read the following encyclopedia article. Then, answer the questions.

**Mythological Stories |** Most cultures have stories from their past. These mythological stories may have some basis in truth but are generally regarded as works of fiction. Myths often describe the origins of people or explain how the universe works.

**Greek Mythology |** The gods and goddesses of Greek mythology are arguably the most famous in the world. In Greek myths, gods and goddesses such as Zeus, Poseidon, Ares, Hera, and Aphrodite frequently involved themselves in the affairs of men. There were also heroes such as Heracles, Theseus, Perseus, Achilles, and Odysseus.

**Roman Mythology |** The Romans adopted many Greek gods and goddesses and gave them new names. Thus Zeus became Jupiter, Athena became Minerva, and Aphrodite became Venus. The Trojan Aeneas became the ancestor of the Romans, and Rome was said to have been founded by the twins Romulus and Remus.

**Norse Mythology |** The Scandinavians in Northern Europe had their own gods and goddesses. Odin was their king while Thor, Freya, and Loki were other deities. They battled giants and enormous monsters such as Fenris Wulf. They believed there would be a great battle at the end of the world called Ragnarok.

**American Mythology |** In more modern times, myths were created about the early American Founding Fathers. There were many about George Washington, the first American president. For instance, when asked by his father if he had chopped down a prized cherry tree with an axe, George responded, "Father, I cannot tell a lie. I did it." Myths like those were told to make the Founding Fathers appear even more impressive.

1 Who are some mythological characters? Do you know any stories about them?

2 Which country's mythology are you the most interested in? Why do you feel that way?

 **Brainstorming** Think about the topic and brainstorm some ideas for your essay. Refer to the words and definitions below for help. Then, answer the questions.

**Building Ideas**

| A Story from Your Country's History | | | |
| --- | --- | --- | --- |
| Person Involved | Event 1 | Event 2 | Event 3 |
| | | | |

**Building Vocabulary**

**legend** *(n)* a nonhistorical story handed down as tradition and often accepted as true

**mythology** *(n)* a collection of ancient stories, which often have a hero or supernatural aspect or which seek to explain a natural phenomenon

**deity** *(n)* a god or goddess

**demigod** *(n)* the son or daughter of a deity and a human

**national hero** *(n)* a person who is considered by the people of a country to have done a great deed for that nation

**tyrant** *(n)* a ruler who is cruel and who often seized power from the rightful ruler

**freedom fighter** *(n)* a person who fights for the freedom of his or her people

**independence** *(n)* freedom

**resist** *(v)* to fight against

**stand up for** *(phr)* to defend a particular person or thing

**rebel** *(v)* to fight against the government or a ruler

**execute** *(v)* to put a person to death; to kill a person

**entertaining** *(adj)* fun; providing pleasure

**fascinating** *(adj)* very interesting

**funny** *(adj)* making one laugh

**famous** *(adj)* very well known

**notorious** *(adj)* well known but often for having done something wrong or bad

**remember** *(v)* to recall; to bring to one's mind

**praise** *(v)* to compliment; to say nice things about

**publicity** *(n)* fame; the act of having people talk or write about a person

**impressive** *(adj)* remarkable

**apocryphal** *(adj)* false; of unlikely or doubtful authorship

**found** *(v)* to establish; to create

*Fill in the blanks with the words above.*

1    Most national heroes are _____ since everyone in the country knows them.

2    The government decided to _____ the rebels and to put them to death.

*Choose the correct words for the sentences.*

3    Everyone laughed because the story was very (impressive / funny).

4    The (tyrant / freedom fighter) controlled the country and ruled ruthlessly.

## Making an Outline

Look at the ideas you came up with in the brainstorming section. Then, use them to create an outline for your essay.

### Introduction

### Body

| Detail 1 | Detail 2 | Detail 3 |
| --- | --- | --- |
| | | |

### Conclusion

## First Draft

Use the outline you wrote above to write the first draft of your essay.

## Appositives

An appositive is a noun or noun phrase positioned next to another noun or noun phrase. The appositive either describes the initial noun or noun phrase or renames it.

For example, you can write the following: *My brother, James, enjoys reading mythology*. In this sentence, *James* is the appositive. Or you could write: *The dog, a stray we found in our backyard, is well trained*. In this sentence, *a stray we found in our backyard* is the appositive.

You can use appositives to shorten your writing. Using an appositive means that you do not have to use a relative clause. For instance, the above sentences could be written "My brother, whose name is James, enjoys reading mythology," and, "The dog, which is a stray we found in our backyard, is well trained." Since it is ideal to omit needless words, appositives can help you do that.

## Model Essay

Read the following sample essay. Underline the appositives.

### William Tell

My country is Switzerland, and William Tell is the most famous man from my nation. He is known as the Swiss national hero of liberty because thanks to him, Switzerland became free.

William Tell lived during the 1300s, when Switzerland was ruled by Duke Gessler, a tyrant. Gessler always demanded that people bow to him. But that was not enough. Once, he put his cap on a tall pole in a public square and insisted that people bow to it. Everyone did that except for one man: William Tell. He proudly walked past the pole.

Gessler became upset, so he had Tell and his son seized. Then, he ordered Tell's son to be put in the middle of the square, and an apple was placed on his head. He told Tell that if he could shoot the arrow off his son's head from 200 paces away, then he could go free.

Tell, an excellent archer, took out an arrow, aimed it, and let it fly. His son did not move an inch as the arrow struck the middle of the apple. As Tell ran to his son, another arrow fell from inside his coat. "Why do you have that second arrow?" asked Gessler. Tell responded, "If I had missed, this second arrow was meant for you." Not long afterward, Tell shot and killed Gessler with an arrow and in doing so, set his country free.

William Tell, one of the bravest men in my country's history, was a great man. Due to his actions, Switzerland became free and has remained that way for centuries.

Use the passive voice to focus on the action, not on the person or thing doing the action. Form the present passive by using "**am/is/are + past participle**" and the past passive by using "**was/were + past participle**."

- William Tell **was disliked** by Gessler.
- The story **is remembered** by everyone in the country.
- Groceries **are sold** at that supermarket.
- The people **were told** to be quiet.

*Write two sentences with "amlislare + past participle" and two sentences with "waslwere + past participle."*

1 ......................................................................................................................................................

2 ......................................................................................................................................................

3 ......................................................................................................................................................

4 ......................................................................................................................................................

*Circle the examples of the passive voice in the essay on the previous page.*

**Self-Evaluation**   Reread your first draft. Then, complete the following self-evaluation.

| | | | |
|---|---|---|---|
| 1 | Did I write a five-paragraph essay? | ☐ YES | ☐ NO |
| 2 | Did I include a thesis statement in the introduction? | ☐ YES | ☐ NO |
| 3 | Did I use examples in each body paragraph? | ☐ YES | ☐ NO |
| 4 | Did I include a topic statement in each body paragraph? | ☐ YES | ☐ NO |
| 5 | Did I restate the thesis statement in the conclusion? | ☐ YES | ☐ NO |
| 6 | Did I use correct grammar? | ☐ YES | ☐ NO |
| 7 | Did I use correct spelling? | ☐ YES | ☐ NO |
| 8 | Did I use correct punctuation? | ☐ YES | ☐ NO |
| 9 | Did I use sequence words properly? | ☐ YES | ☐ NO |
| 10 | Did I use transition words well? | ☐ YES | ☐ NO |
| 11 | Did I avoid using contractions? | ☐ YES | ☐ NO |
| 12 | Did I make logical arguments? | ☐ YES | ☐ NO |

**Final Draft**   Now, using the self-evaluation, write your final draft.

---

**Evaluate Your Partner's Essay**   Read your partner's essay and make positive and negative comments on it. Use the self-evaluation form on the previous page if you need help.

**Choose the Best Essay**   Divide into groups of four and read all of the essays. Then, decide which essay is the best. Discuss why you feel that way with your group members.

Look at the following topics. Choose one of them and write a narrative essay.

**More Topics**

- What is your favorite story about a mythological hero?

- What is your country's foundation story?

- Can you describe an important event in your country's past?

- What is one of the greatest events that has happened during your lifetime?

- Can you describe an imaginary future event that you would like to see happen in your country?

# 17 A Scary Moment in Your Life

**WRITING ASSIGNMENT**

What was something scary that happened to you? Where were you when it took place? Why did it scare you so much?

## Building Background

Read the following announcement. Then, answer the questions.

### The Fulton County Theater is proudly sponsoring Horror Film Week

**Tuesday, October 26: *Night of the Living Dead***
Come to see one of the best zombie movies of all time. This movie has become a cult classic, and you will definitely be frightened during the screening of this film.

**Wednesday, October 27: *Aliens***
Join Sigourney Weaver as she and a group of space marines take on some virtually unstoppable aliens. You'll be praying that aliens aren't real while you're watching this film.

**Thursday, October 28: *The Exorcist***
This movie about demonic possession is considered one of the scariest movies ever. Watch as priests do battle against evil to exorcise a demon.

**Friday, October 29: *The Silence of the Lambs***
Anthony Hopkins stars as Hannibal Lector, a murderous cannibal serial killer who provides assistance to Jodie Foster, who plays an FBI agent seeking to stop another serial killer.

**Saturday, October 30: *A Nightmare on Elm Street***
After watching this film, you won't want to fall asleep again. Be sure to see what happens when Freddy Kruger invades people's dreams. It's not pleasant.

**Sunday, October 31: Halloween**
Michael Meyers has escaped from an insane asylum, and he's looking for his long-lost sister. This is one of the greatest slasher films ever. Don't miss it.

1   What is the topic of each movie? What are some other movies with similar topics?

2   What do you think of horror movies? What was the last scary movie that you saw?

**Brainstorming** Think about the topic and brainstorm some ideas for your essay. Refer to the words and definitions below for help. Then, answer the questions.

## Building Ideas

| A Scary Moment in My Life | | | |
| --- | --- | --- | --- |
| When and Where | Event 1 | Event 2 | Event 3 |
| | | | |

## Building Vocabulary

**frighten** *(v)* to scare someone

**scared** *(adj)* experiencing fear

**crime** *(n)* an illegal act

**criminal** *(n)* a person who engages in an illegal act or acts

**robbery** *(n)* the act of stealing something

**threat** *(n)* a statement of one's intentions to cause harm to another person

**violent** *(adj)* acting with extreme force

**weapon** *(n)* any kind of tool that is used to cause harm to someone

**murderer** *(n)* a person who kills another individual

**arson** *(n)* the act of setting a fire and burning something intentionally

**danger** *(n)* exposure to something that could cause harm

**dangerous** *(adj)* able to cause harm

**accident** *(n)* an event that happens unintentionally and often causes harm to people or things

**crash** *(n)* an event in which a vehicle collides with someone or something, which often results in harm or damage of some sort

**drunk driving** *(n)* the act of driving after one has had too many alcoholic drinks

**home invasion** *(n)* the act of illegally entering someone's house with the intention of causing harm to the person or people in the house

**power outage** *(n)* an event when electricity stops working

**storm** *(n)* a very strong rainstorm

**typhoon** *(n)* a powerful tropical rainstorm that often results in heavy rain and winds

**flood** *(n)* an event in which the level of a river, lake, sea, or ocean rises so that water covers land

**earthquake** *(n)* the sudden and often violent shaking of the ground

**natural disaster** *(n)* an event such as a flood, tornado, or storm that happens and which causes damage

**catastrophe** *(n)* an event that causes great damage, pain, and suffering

**injure** *(v)* to harm or hurt someone

**wound** *(n)* an injury that often involves the skin being cut and a person bleeding

*Fill in the blanks with the words above.*

1   The _____ at the bank resulted in the theft of several thousand dollars.

2   If you have too many beers, please do not engage in _____ .

*Choose the correct words for the sentences.*

3   Many people were (scared / dangerous) when they saw the horror film.

4   We were almost involved in a car (crash / catastrophe) with another vehicle.

## Making an Outline

Look at the ideas you came up with in the brainstorming section. Then, use them to create an outline for your essay.

### Introduction

### Body

| Detail 1 | Detail 2 | Detail 3 |
| --- | --- | --- |
| | | |

### Conclusion

## First Draft

Use the outline you wrote above to write the first draft of your essay.

## Quotations

Quotations are records of the exact words that people say. When you are writing a narrative essay, there are many times when you may need to quote the words people said.

To quote others, you need to use quotation marks (" ") before and after the quoted speech. Their presence indicates that you are quoting exact speech. Be sure to use double quotation marks, not single quotation marks. Before the quoted part, you should use *say, speak, talk, ask, answer, reply, shout, yell,* or other words that indicate speech.

You need to use precise punctuation when making quotations. Here are some examples:

He said, "That was really scary." / "That was really scary," he said.
He asked, "Was that really scary?" / "Was that really scary?" he asked.

 **Model Essay**   Read the following sample essay. Underline the quotations.

### The Scariest Moment

I have not had very many scary moments in my life. However, there is one frightening event during a family trip that stands out in my mind.

Two years ago, my family went on a vacation to Australia, where we spent lots of time on the beach. One day, we decided to go snorkeling, so we bought tickets for a snorkeling trip and took a boat out to a coral reef in the ocean.

I was having a great time snorkeling and looking at all kinds of beautiful fish. Then, I heard some screaming. I put my head up out of the water and heard people shouting, "Get out of the water!" I looked around and saw some people on the boat pointing near me. I looked to where they were pointing and saw a huge fin above the water. It was a shark!

I could not believe my eyes. I immediately started swimming toward the boat. Everyone was yelling, "Hurry! Hurry!" I looked and saw that the fin was getting closer. By this time, I was the only person in the water. As I reached the boat, my father said, "Take my hand," and he reached down, grabbed my hand, and pulled me out of the water. Just then, an enormous shark swam right by the boat.

Having a close encounter with a shark was the scariest moment in my life. I could have been eaten by the shark, but thanks to my father and other people, I managed to survive.

**Grammar in Writing**

**Imperatives** are commands or orders. The subject of an imperative is *you*, but you do not use *you* in the sentence. Instead, omit it. So instead of using, "You go home," write, "Go home." Instead of using, "You be careful!" write, "Be careful." Use "do not + verb" to make negative imperatives.

- **Tell** me about a scary time in your life.
- **Come** back home and **eat** dinner now.
- **Do not stay** out until late at night.
- **Do not watch** that horror movie.

*Write two imperative sentences and two negative imperative sentences.*

1 _____

2 _____

3 _____

4 _____

*Circle the imperative sentences in the essay on the previous page.*

**Self-Evaluation**   Reread your first draft. Then, complete the following self-evaluation.

| | | | |
|---|---|---|---|
| 1 | Did I write a five-paragraph essay? | ☐ YES | ☐ NO |
| 2 | Did I include a thesis statement in the introduction? | ☐ YES | ☐ NO |
| 3 | Did I use examples in each body paragraph? | ☐ YES | ☐ NO |
| 4 | Did I include a topic statement in each body paragraph? | ☐ YES | ☐ NO |
| 5 | Did I restate the thesis statement in the conclusion? | ☐ YES | ☐ NO |
| 6 | Did I use correct grammar? | ☐ YES | ☐ NO |
| 7 | Did I use correct spelling? | ☐ YES | ☐ NO |
| 8 | Did I use correct punctuation? | ☐ YES | ☐ NO |
| 9 | Did I use sequence words properly? | ☐ YES | ☐ NO |
| 10 | Did I use transition words well? | ☐ YES | ☐ NO |
| 11 | Did I avoid using contractions? | ☐ YES | ☐ NO |
| 12 | Did I make logical arguments? | ☐ YES | ☐ NO |

**Final Draft**    Now, using the self-evaluation, write your final draft.

_____

_____

_____

_____

_____

_____

_____

_____

_____

_____

_____

**Evaluate Your Partner's Essay**    Read your partner's essay and make positive and negative comments on it. Use the self-evaluation form on the previous page if you need help.

**Choose the Best Essay**    Divide into groups of four and read all of the essays. Then, decide which essay is the best. Discuss why you feel that way with your group members.

Look at the following topics. Choose one of them and write a narrative essay.

- Describe the story in your favorite horror movie.
- Do you know any urban legends from your culture? What is one of them?
- What were you scared of when you were a child? What happened that made you scared of that particular thing?
- Have your parents ever told you any scary instances they were involved in? Can you describe one?
- What is your biggest fear? What do you think would happen if that fear were realized?

**More Topics**

# A Time When You Helped Someone

**WRITING ASSIGNMENT**

When did you help someone in the past? What kind of assistance did the person need? How did you help that person? What were the results?

## Building Background

Read the following advertisement. Then, answer the questions.

### Become a Volunteer
### and
### Help Your Fellow Residents

How would you like to make the city of Amity better? You can do that by becoming a volunteer. You won't get paid anything, but you'll experience the joy of knowing that you helped others and improved their lives in some way. Here are some of the ways you can volunteer to improve Amity:

**Library**: Volunteer at the library by putting books back on the shelves and by helping people find reading material. You can also spend time reading books to young children if you want to help them out.

**Hospital**: The doctors and nurses at local hospitals could always use volunteers. You'll get to help take care of patients as well as their friends and family members who are visiting them.

**Animal Shelter**: Do you like animals? The lost, neglected, and abused animals at our local animal shelters would love to have volunteers spend time with them. Play with the animals, bathe them, walk them, and feed them.

**Soup Kitchen**: The homeless and poor in our community sometimes drop by the soup kitchen to get hot meals. Lend a hand by cooking food, serving food, cleaning off tables, or washing dishes.

**Trash Collection**: The city's parks and roads sometimes get covered with litter, so we need people who can help us pick it up and throw it out. This is a great opportunity for people who enjoy spending time outdoors and want to see Amity become as beautiful as possible.

1    Which places need volunteers? What kind of assistance does each place require?

2    Have you ever volunteered? What kind of volunteer work did you do in the past?

**Brainstorming** Think about the topic and brainstorm some ideas for your essay. Refer to the words and definitions below for help. Then, answer the questions.

**Building Ideas**

| A Time When I Helped Someone | | | |
| --- | --- | --- | --- |
| When and Where | Who | Situation | Action |
| | | | |

**Building Vocabulary**

**assist** (v) to help someone do something

**assistance** (n) help

**volunteer** (n) a person who works for free, often in order to help others

**orphan** (n) a child with no parents

**orphanage** (n) a place in which many orphans live together

**aide** (n) an assistant; a person who provides help

**donate** (v) to give something such as money to help others

**donation** (n) a gift such as money that is intended to help others

**charity** (n) an organization whose goal is to help others

**dedicated** (adj) committed to something such as personal or political goal

**devote** (v) to focus on a specific goal or pursuit

**considerate** (adj) being mindful of others' thoughts or feelings

**generous** (adj) giving; sharing; unselfish

**thoughtful** (adj) showing consideration toward others

**appreciate** (v) to be grateful or thankful for

**appreciative** (adj) grateful; thankful

**regret** (v) to feel bad about something that happened in the past and to hope that it had not happened

**wish** (v) to hope that something will happen in the future

**loan** (n) money that a person gives to another with the expectation that it will be paid back later

**lend** (v) to give money or something else to a person with the expectation that it will be paid back or returned later

**borrow** (v) to take money or something else from a person with the expectation of paying it back or returning it later

**destitute** (adj) deprived of or lacking something such as food, money, or shelter

**bankrupt** (adj) having no money

**fail** (v) not to succeed at doing something

**tutor** (n) a person who teaches another person on an individual basis

*Fill in the blanks with the words above.*

1 She has _____ her life to assisting people in need.

2 His company suddenly went _____ , so he became destitute.

*Choose the correct words for the sentences.*

3 I would love to (borrow / lend) you some money, but I cannot do that today.

4 The large (donation / charity) to the orphanage was appreciated by everyone.

## Making an Outline

Look at the ideas you came up with in the brainstorming section. Then, use them to create an outline for your essay.

### Introduction

### Body

| Detail 1 | Detail 2 | Detail 3 |
| --- | --- | --- |

### Conclusion

## First Draft

Use the outline you wrote above to write the first draft of your essay.

## How to Make Your Writing Better

## Familiar and Unfamiliar Words

You need to select the words in your essay carefully. In most cases, it is better to use familiar words than unfamiliar words. Familiar words are those which most readers know and understand. Unfamiliar words are those words which most readers neither know nor understand.

The problem with unfamiliar words is that readers may have to stop to think about the meanings of the words. In some cases, they may need to look up the words in the dictionary to figure out what they mean. When that happens, the flow of the essay is interrupted, so readers often enjoy the essay less and do not learn as much from it as possible.

While you do not want to use only simple and easy words, you should avoid using words that are very high in level. These unfamiliar words detract from your essay and often annoy readers.

**Model Essay**    Read the following sample essay. Underline the unfamiliar words.

### A Time When I Helped Someone

I like to help people whenever I have the opportunity to do so. A few years ago, I had the chance to assist my sister when she required some succor.

I had been saving my money because I wanted to purchase a new car. I almost had enough money, so I was starting to consider which kind of car I should procure for myself. Then, my parents gave me some information about my sister. Apparently, she was thinking about dropping out of college because she could not afford the tuition anymore.

I called her up and talked to her about her problem. She informed me that her school had amplified the price of tuition, so it was unaffordable for her. Even worse, she was just one semester away from graduation. Right there, I decided to give my sister the money she needed to afford school.

She was euphoric. She gladly accepted my offer and then went on to graduate from college. After that, she managed to find a great job that helped her get started on her career. A year later, she paid me back the lucre even though I had told her that it was a gift. I felt great about being able to help my sister since it let her have a successful life.

Helping my sister when she needed the money stands out in my mind as a time when I helped someone. I was able to assist someone who needed help, and she truly appreciated it.

**Grammar in Writing**

An **infinitive** is the base form of a verb preceded by the word *to*. After some verbs, you need to use an infinitive if you want to include a second verb. Some verbs that are followed by infinitives are *want, have, need, decide, manage, hope, desire, agree, love,* and *hate*.

- Mr. Reeves **loves to help** people in need.
- You **have to be** careful when you drive.
- They **agreed to meet** again the following week.
- We **decided to volunteer** at the local hospital.

*Write two sentences with "to + verb" that follow a present tense verb and two sentences with "to + verb" that follow a past tense verb.*

1 .................................................................................................................................

2 .................................................................................................................................

3 .................................................................................................................................

4 .................................................................................................................................

*Circle the examples of "to + verb" that follow a verb in the essay on the previous page.*

**Self-Evaluation**   Reread your first draft. Then, complete the following self-evaluation.

| | | |
|---|---|---|
| 1 | Did I write a five-paragraph essay? | ☐ YES ☐ NO |
| 2 | Did I include a thesis statement in the introduction? | ☐ YES ☐ NO |
| 3 | Did I use examples in each body paragraph? | ☐ YES ☐ NO |
| 4 | Did I include a topic statement in each body paragraph? | ☐ YES ☐ NO |
| 5 | Did I restate the thesis statement in the conclusion? | ☐ YES ☐ NO |
| 6 | Did I use correct grammar? | ☐ YES ☐ NO |
| 7 | Did I use correct spelling? | ☐ YES ☐ NO |
| 8 | Did I use correct punctuation? | ☐ YES ☐ NO |
| 9 | Did I use sequence words properly? | ☐ YES ☐ NO |
| 10 | Did I use transition words well? | ☐ YES ☐ NO |
| 11 | Did I avoid using contractions? | ☐ YES ☐ NO |
| 12 | Did I make logical arguments? | ☐ YES ☐ NO |

**Final Draft**  Now, using the self-evaluation, write your final draft.

**Evaluate Your Partner's Essay**  Read your partner's essay and make positive and negative comments on it. Use the self-evaluation form on the previous page if you need help.

**Choose the Best Essay**  Divide into groups of four and read all of the essays. Then, decide which essay is the best. Discuss why you feel that way with your group members.

Look at the following topics. Choose one of them and write a narrative essay.

**More Topics**

- Write about a time when someone helped you.

- Have you ever wanted to help someone but did not do so? What happened?

- How would you like to assist someone in the future?

- Has anyone in your family gotten assistance from someone else? Can you explain what happened?

- Do you know any stories in your country's history of when one person helped another? Describe what happened.

# 19 The Last Trip You Took

**WRITING ASSIGNMENT**

What was the last trip you took? When and where did you go? What activities did you do on that trip? Can you describe some of the highlights of your trip?

## Building Background

Read the following pamphlet. Then, answer the questions.

## Book the Trip of a Lifetime

We at Global Travel have been serving the needs of domestic and foreign travelers for three decades. Book one of our package tours or let us design the trip of a lifetime for you. Here are some of the special deals we are currently offering:

**Amazon Adventure**: Spend 8 days and 9 nights in the heart of the Amazon Rainforest. Go trekking through the jungle and rafting down the river. You'll see all sorts of exotic wildlife and learn about one of the world's most vital ecosystems.

**The Silk Road**: Retrace the ancient trade route that went from China to Rome. For 2 weeks, you'll spend time in China, India, the Middle East, and Italy. You'll travel by air, land, and sea and will visit some of the world's oldest cities on this tour.

**African Safari**: Spend 5 days and 4 nights in Kenya, where you'll see exotic animals on the Serengeti. You'll watch enormous herds of zebras and wildebeests as they make their great migration, and you'll have the opportunity to see elephants, rhinos, and various great cats as you camp in the wild.

**European Castles**: Interested in seeing some of the world's most beautiful medieval castles? Then this trip is for you. You'll visit castles in England, France, Germany, and Italy, and you'll even be able to spend the night in several of them. This is an ideal trip for lovers of history.

Call 891-9276 to learn more about our trips and to inquire about prices.

1   Where does each trip go? What activities can people do on each trip?

2   Which of these trips would you like to go on the most? Why do you feel that way?

## Brainstorming

Think about the topic and brainstorm some ideas for your essay. Refer to the words and definitions below for help. Then, answer the questions.

### Building Ideas

| The Last Trip I Took | | | |
|---|---|---|---|
| When and Where | Activity 1 | Activity 2 | Activity 3 |
| | | | |

### Building Vocabulary

**budget** (n) the amount of money a person can spend on something

**book** (v) to reserve something such as a ticket, hotel room, or rental car

**accommodations** (n) a place where a person can spend the night *used in the plural form

**delay** (n) the act of putting off something until a later time

**cancelation** (n) the act of calling off a planned event

**vacancy** (n) available space, such as a room at a hotel or a table at a restaurant

**change in plans** (phr) an instance where a scheduled activity is not done in favor of doing something else

**dream trip** (n) a trip that a person has been looking forward to doing for a long time; a trip that a person expects will never be equaled

**domestic** (adj) relating to within one's own country

**enjoyable** (adj) fun

**bargain** (n) a great deal, such as a quality item available for a low price

**rip-off** (n) something that costs too much and is often of low quality

**con artist** (n) a person who tries to cheat others out of their money

**rob** (v) to steal something from another person

**lose one's way** (phr) to be unable to find one's destination

**shortcut** (n) a way that is faster than the route which one is following

**five-star hotel** (n) an expensive, exclusive hotel better than almost all other types of places to stay at

**exhausted** (adj) extremely tired

**refreshed** (adj) feeling rested and energized

**thrilling** (adj) very exciting

**horrible** (adj) terrible; very bad

**misunderstand** (v) to think a person means one thing when that person actually means something else

**translation** (n) the act of changing words from one language to another

**interpreter** (n) a person who can change words from one language to another

*Fill in the blanks with the words above.*

1    The _____ of all flights when the airport was shut down made us have to take the train.

2    They would rather stay at a _____ than save money by staying somewhere cheap.

*Choose the correct words for the sentences.*

3    We need an accurate (interpreter / translation) of these documents.

4    I feel (refreshed / horrible) after spending a relaxing week at the beach.

## Making an Outline

Look at the ideas you came up with in the brainstorming section. Then, use them to create an outline for your essay.

| Introduction |
|---|
|  |

| Body | | |
|---|---|---|
| Detail 1 | Detail 2 | Detail 3 |
|  |  |  |

| Conclusion |
|---|
|  |

## First Draft

Use the outline you wrote above to write the first draft of your essay.

## Types of Sentences

When writing an essay, you want to use a variety of types of sentences. If you use the same sentence types over and over again, your essay will be boring to read. By using different sentence forms, your writing will be more interesting.

The most basic type of sentence is the simple sentence. This sentence contains a subject and a verb. It also expresses a complete thought and only has one clause. *I went to the park* and *Joe lives in Australia* are simple sentences.

A compound sentence has two or more independent clauses. And independent clause contains a subject and a verb and can stand alone as a sentence. The independent clauses are joined by a coordinating conjunction such as *and, but, or, yet, so,* and *for. She took a trip, and she had fun* and *My brother is a lawyer, so he is busy* are compound sentences.

A complex sentence contains one independent clause and one or more dependent clauses. A dependent clause cannot stand alone as a sentence. A complex sentence also includes a subordinating conjunction such as *because, when, while,* and *although. Because we traveled together, we felt safe* is a complex sentence.

Combine these three sentence types to make writing that flows well. Avoid using too many of the same types of sentences in a row. By varying the sentence types, your essay will improve in both quality and style.

 **Model Essay** Read the following sample essay. Underline the compound sentences and put brackets [~] around the complex sentences.

## My Last Trip

Last summer, my family decided to take a trip because we had not gone anywhere together for a long time. We thought about traveling abroad or going to the beach, but we decided to go camping instead.

There is a national park about two hours away from our home, so we packed our camping equipment, drove to the park, and went hiking in the woods. We found a nice place to pitch our tent near a lake and then started collecting wood to make a fire at night.

On the first day, we hiked in the forest and went fishing in the lake. We caught a few fish, so we planned to cook them for dinner. Fish roasted over an open fire tastes delicious. When night came, we sat around the campfire, talked about our lives, and told some stories.

The next three days were similar to the first one. We had a mostly relaxing time and became really close to one another on our trip. Of course, camping in the woods was hard, and we got bitten by lots of bugs, but overall, we were all incredibly happy when it was time to pack up everything and drive back home.

I had a great time on my last trip. Camping in the forest with my family for a few days was a wonderful experience. I hope that all of my trips in the future are as good as it was.

A predicate is the part of a sentence that includes the verb and any objects, complements, or other parts of speech. A **compound predicate** includes two or more verbs that modify the same subject.

- We often **eat** and **drink** at that restaurant.
- She **studied** and **worked** yesterday.
- I **bought** a ticket and **took** a trip.
- David **will call** his friend and **speak** with him.

*Write four sentences with a compound predicate.*

1 _____

2 _____

3 _____

4 _____

*Circle the verbs in the compound predicates in the essay on the previous page.*

## Self-Evaluation    Reread your first draft. Then, complete the following self-evaluation.

| | | | |
|---|---|---|---|
| 1 | Did I write a five-paragraph essay? | ☐ YES | ☐ NO |
| 2 | Did I include a thesis statement in the introduction? | ☐ YES | ☐ NO |
| 3 | Did I use examples in each body paragraph? | ☐ YES | ☐ NO |
| 4 | Did I include a topic statement in each body paragraph? | ☐ YES | ☐ NO |
| 5 | Did I restate the thesis statement in the conclusion? | ☐ YES | ☐ NO |
| 6 | Did I use correct grammar? | ☐ YES | ☐ NO |
| 7 | Did I use correct spelling? | ☐ YES | ☐ NO |
| 8 | Did I use correct punctuation? | ☐ YES | ☐ NO |
| 9 | Did I use sequence words properly? | ☐ YES | ☐ NO |
| 10 | Did I use transition words well? | ☐ YES | ☐ NO |
| 11 | Did I avoid using contractions? | ☐ YES | ☐ NO |
| 12 | Did I make logical arguments? | ☐ YES | ☐ NO |

**Final Draft** Now, using the self-evaluation, write your final draft.

**Evaluate Your Partner's Essay**

Read your partner's essay and make positive and negative comments on it. Use the self-evaluation form on the previous page if you need help.

**Choose the Best Essay**

Divide into groups of four and read all of the essays. Then, decide which essay is the best. Discuss why you feel that way with your group members.

Look at the following topics. Choose one of them and write a narrative essay.

**More Topics**

- What is your dream trip? What will you do on that trip?

- Have you ever been on a trip abroad? What did you do?

- What was a problem that happened on a trip you took? Describe what happened.

- Have you ever gotten hurt or sick on a trip? Write about what happened.

- Have any of your friends had unique experiences on trips they took? Can you describe what happened to them?

# UNIT 20

# A Time You Learned a Valuable Lesson

**WRITING ASSIGNMENT**

When was a time in your life that you learned a valuable lesson? What happened then? What was the lesson that you learned? How did that event change your life?

## Building Background

Read the following comments on a blog. Then, answer the questions.

---

**5 Comments**

Share ➔  Favorite ★

**David Ramsey**  *5 hours ago*

Thanks for sharing that personal story with us, Mark. I'm sure this will be a life-changing moment for you. I remember when my father passed away about ten years ago. It was right then that I realized how short life is. Since that time, I've spent as much time as possible with my family and have become a better father to my children and a better husband to my wife.

**Meredith Franklin**  *4 hours ago*

Touching story, Mark. I had a similar experience happen to me. After my car accident, I understood that I could have been seriously injured or even killed. I make sure to tell my family members how much I love them since any moment could be my last.

**Gregory Mason**  *2 hours ago*

I haven't had any life-threatening moments, but I remember making my little sister cry when I broke her favorite toy on purpose. I'll never forget the look on her face. She was mad at me for weeks, and I deserved that. Even though I immediately became a nicer brother, she didn't trust me for a long time afterward.

**Sophia Popov**  *20 minutes ago*

Like Gregory, nothing too bad has happened to me. But I remember cheating on a test once in high school. Although I didn't get caught, I knew deep down inside that I'd done something wrong. I confessed to my teacher and accepted the punishment he gave me. I've never felt like cheating again even when I knew I was going to do poorly on an exam.

---

1   What life-changing moment did each of the commenters have?

2   Which of the above life-changing moments can you relate to the most? What event from your life is similar to the events in the comments?

**Brainstorming** Think about the topic and brainstorm some ideas for your essay. Refer to the words and definitions below for help. Then, answer the questions.

## Building Ideas

| A Time I Learned a Valuable Lesson | | | |
|---|---|---|---|
| When and Where | Situation | Result | Actions |
| | | | |

## Building Vocabulary

**near-death experience** *(n)* a time when a person almost dies for some reason

**collision** *(n)* an incident when two or more objects, such as vehicles, run into or hit each other

**wreck** *(n)* the result of a crash or similar accident

**life-threatening** *(adj)* endangering the life of a person

**severe** *(adj)* very serious

**consideration** *(n)* the act of thinking about other people and how they feel

**selfish** *(adj)* being greedy and wanting things only for oneself

**selfless** *(adj)* being generous and willing to share or to help others

**laziness** *(n)* the act or feeling of not wanting to do work or any type of physical activity

**debt** *(n)* money owed to someone else

**spendthrift** *(n)* a person who likes to spend lots of money

**shopping spree** *(n)* an occasion when a person spends a lot of money to buy many items while shopping

**careless** *(adj)* not paying close attention to what one is doing

**friendship** *(n)* the state of being close to another person

**anger** *(n)* a strong feeling of displeasure

**pride** *(n)* a high opinion of oneself

**egotism** *(n)* self-centeredness

**narcissist** *(n)* a person who loves oneself very much

**passion** *(n)* a powerful or strong emotion

**risk** *(n)* danger

**cowardice** *(n)* a feeling of being afraid of something or fearful of doing something

**bravery** *(n)* courage

**honest** *(adj)* upright; fair; truthful

**lie** *(v)* to make a statement that is not true

**liar** *(n)* a person who tells lies

*Fill in the blanks with the words above.*

1   He has no _____ for the feelings of others most of the time.

2   Jennifer spent more than $2,000 on her latest _____ .

*Choose the correct words for the sentences.*

3   Thank to his (narcissist / bravery), the solider was able to win the fight.

4   Only a (selfish / selfless) person does not want to share with others.

## Making an Outline

Look at the ideas you came up with in the brainstorming section. Then, use them to create an outline for your essay.

### Introduction

### Body

| Detail 1 | Detail 2 | Detail 3 |
| --- | --- | --- |

### Conclusion

## First Draft

Use the outline you wrote above to write the first draft of your essay.

## Avoiding Repetition

When writing an essay, try to avoid repetition. If you use the same words and phrases over and over, the quality of your essay will be poor.

To avoid repetition, read each sentence carefully to make sure you do not use the same word twice in the sentence. Words like *a, an, the,* and the *be* verb can be repeated, but words with more than two syllables should not appear twice in the same sentence unless it simply cannot be avoided. For instance, *Actually, I was actually about to call you* contains the word *actually* twice. Delete one usage of it to avoid repetition.

You should also make sure you do not start too many sentences with the same word or words. Some people begin numerous sentences in their essays with words such as *because, in addition,* and *however*. If you do that too many times, your writing will suffer in quality.

Finally, remember that pronouns are your friends. If you mention a noun in one sentence, you do not always need to repeat it in the following sentence. Just use a pronoun to avoid repetition. For instance, rather than writing *I met my friend. My friend lives near me*, you should write *I met my friend. She lives near me*. It is safe to assume that your readers will know who or what you are referring to, so make effective use of pronouns.

**Model Essay**   Read the following sample essay. Underline the parts that use repetition.

### A Lesson I Learned

There have been several events in my life when I learned important lessons. One event happened when I was a middle school student. Because of that time in middle school, I changed how I treated people.

Once, my class took a math test. Mathematics happened to be my best subject, so I did very well on the test. In fact, when the teacher returned the tests, I received a perfect score, but my best friend got an F because she had not studied. When I saw her grade, I started laughing, making her burst into tears.

A month later, my class took a history test. I did really poorly on the history test, but my best friend did not. However, when she saw how upset I was, she did not laugh at me. Instead, she comforted me and told me that it was all right and that I would do better the next time.

I immediately remembered how I had treated her. I felt awful about my treatment of her, so I immediately apologized. She graciously accepted my apology. From that incident, I learned the importance of being sympathetic to others. Rather than laughing at people when something bad happens, I needed to help them feel better.

Since then, I no longer make fun of people when they do poorly at something. Instead, I encourage them and help them gain confidence. That incident at school has remained in my memory for years, and it was definitely an important lesson I learned at school.

**Grammar in Writing**

Use "**rather than + verb**" or "**rather than + verb -ing**" to indicate that instead of doing one activity, a person does or wants to do a different one.

- **Rather than get** mad at me, my friend stayed calm.
- I will watch a movie **rather than stay** at home.
- **Rather than eating** now, we are having dinner later.
- They are studying **rather than going** out.

*Write two sentences with "rather than + verb" and two sentences with "rather than + verb -ing."*

1
2
3
4

*Circle "rather than" in the essay on the previous page.*

**Self-Evaluation**   Reread your first draft. Then, complete the following self-evaluation.

| | | | |
|---|---|---|---|
| 1 | Did I write a five-paragraph essay? | ☐ YES | ☐ NO |
| 2 | Did I include a thesis statement in the introduction? | ☐ YES | ☐ NO |
| 3 | Did I use examples in each body paragraph? | ☐ YES | ☐ NO |
| 4 | Did I include a topic statement in each body paragraph? | ☐ YES | ☐ NO |
| 5 | Did I restate the thesis statement in the conclusion? | ☐ YES | ☐ NO |
| 6 | Did I use correct grammar? | ☐ YES | ☐ NO |
| 7 | Did I use correct spelling? | ☐ YES | ☐ NO |
| 8 | Did I use correct punctuation? | ☐ YES | ☐ NO |
| 9 | Did I use sequence words properly? | ☐ YES | ☐ NO |
| 10 | Did I use transition words well? | ☐ YES | ☐ NO |
| 11 | Did I avoid using contractions? | ☐ YES | ☐ NO |
| 12 | Did I make logical arguments? | ☐ YES | ☐ NO |

**Final Draft** Now, using the self-evaluation, write your final draft.

**Evaluate Your Partner's Essay**

Read your partner's essay and make positive and negative comments on it. Use the self-evaluation form on the previous page if you need help.

**Choose the Best Essay**

Divide into groups of four and read all of the essays. Then, decide which essay is the best. Discuss why you feel that way with your group members.

Look at the following topics. Choose one of them and write a narrative essay.

**More Topics**

- Have you ever had a near-death experience? What happened?
- Do you know any fables that teach a valuable lesson? What is the story, and what is the lesson?
- Is there an example from your country's history of a person who learned a valuable lesson?
- Have you ever suddenly changed a bad habit into a good one? What caused you to do that?
- When was a time that you treated a person poorly? What happened, and why did you do that?

# Answer Key

# 01 UNIT My Neighborhood in Thirty Years

## Building Vocabulary p.12

1  monorails
2  vertical farms
3  Suburban
4  carpool

## Model Essay and Grammar in Writing p.14

### My Neighborhood Thirty Years from Now

I live downtown in a large urban center. Thirty years from now, my neighborhood will look much different from today. The three main differences will be the sizes of the buildings, the types of transportation people use, and the way the Internet of Things will affect my neighborhood.

First, the buildings will be larger than today. Right now, my neighborhood has some large buildings. But there will be many buildings more than 100 stories high three decades from now. Building methods will improve, making it easier and faster to construct large buildings. People will live, work, and shop in these buildings.

Second, the methods of transportation used in my neighborhood are going to change. Most people in my neighborhood drive cars or ride on buses. In the future, fewer cars are going to be on the road. Instead, people are going to use buses and ride in monorails above the roads. For pedestrians, moving sidewalks are going to transport them from one place to another quickly.

Third, the Internet of Things will greatly improve my neighborhood. When a person is walking alone at night, streetlights will turn on to guide that person home safely. Buses will appear at bus stops when enough people are waiting for them. And when trashcans are full, the government will be alerted automatically. Then, garbage trucks will arrive to keep the neighborhood clean.

These are just a few of the changes that will happen in my neighborhood in thirty years. These changes will make my neighborhood a much better place to live. So more people will want to live there.

## 02 UNIT How to Improve Your Health

## Building Vocabulary p.18

1  routine
2  underweight
3  depression
4  Obese

## Model Essay and Grammar in Writing p.20

### How to Improve My Health

I am a healthy person in general. However, there are several ways I can improve my health. I will discuss three in this essay. The ways to improve my health are to change my eating habits, to exercise more, and to reduce my stress. Let me explain how I can do each of these activities.

First of all, I have to change my eating habits by consuming more nutritious food. Currently, I eat too much fast food and enjoy sugary snacks such as chocolate and candy bars. I ought to stop eating all of that junk food and start eating better food. I plan to eat more vegetables, especially leafy green ones like lettuce and broccoli. I must also eat more fruits, nuts, and healthy meat such as fish.

The next way I intend to improve my health is to exercise more often. I sometimes play sports at the park with my friends, but that is not sufficient. I should exercise for thirty minutes each day at least five days a week. I want to do a combination of exercises so that I can improve my strength and flexibility and enhance my cardiovascular system.

Finally, I absolutely must reduce the stress in my life. I am a student, so I study constantly and also worry about my grades all the time. To lower my stress level, I can do many things. I should get more sleep and meditate while I am awake. I should also try to have some fun by going out with my friends.

If I can do those three activities, I can improve my health a great deal. That will allow me to have a better, happier, and healthier life.

## 03 UNIT How to Be a Good Friend

## Building Vocabulary p.24

1  favor
2  silence
3  keep a secret
4  warmhearted

## Model Essay and Grammar in Writing p.26

### How to Be a Good Friend

Have you ever wondered how to be a good friend? I used to be friendless, and it really bothered me. Then, I did some research and realized that being a good friend requires just a few special steps. For me, being a good listener, being trustworthy, and engaging in give and take were vital to becoming a good friend.

People love talking about themselves, so a good friend should be a good listener. I was once a big talker who loved telling people about myself, but nobody wanted to listen to me. When I started being quiet and listening to others, I acquired more friends. Few people listen well, so good listeners are highly valued as friends.

Next, it is crucial to be a trustworthy person. I lost countless friends in the past because I could not keep their secrets. If somebody told me a secret, I immediately blabbed about it to others. I realized I had to become more trustworthy. People learned they could speak to me in confidence, and I would not tell others anything.

Finally, there must be give and take for a relationship to be successful. When people did favors for me, I never returned their kindness. But friends do not act that way, so I changed my ways. Now, when a friend does something nice for me, I return the favor by doing something nice for that friend.

Being a good friend is not difficult. You simply need to listen to others and avoid talking about yourself too much. In addition, be trustworthy and engage in give and take. Follow those three simple steps, and you can be a good friend.

# UNIT 04 The Water Cycle

## Building Vocabulary p.30

| | |
|---|---|
| 1 purify | 2 accumulate |
| 3 precipitation | 4 dust |

## Model Essay and Grammar in Writing p.32

### The Water Cycle

The water cycle refers to the circulation of water in its solid, liquid, and gaseous forms around the Earth. Because water is vital to all life, a thorough understanding of the water cycle is important. There are four basic steps involved in it: evaporation, condensation, precipitation, and collection.

When water evaporates, it changes from a liquid into its gaseous form, called water vapor. Evaporation takes place due to the sun's heat. Heat from the sun causes water in various bodies of water to evaporate.

Water vapor is so small that people cannot see it. Water vapor slowly rises into the air. At some point, the air temperature becomes cold enough that water vapor changes into liquid form once again. This is called condensation. When water condenses, there are small droplets of water in the air. They often combine to form clouds.

The next stage is precipitation. When clouds release the water in them, it falls to the ground as rain, snow, sleet, hail, or ice. This water may be absorbed into the ground. It may also fall into oceans, seas, rivers, lakes, and other bodies of water and be collected there. This is the final stage of the water cycle. Once collection occurs, evaporation can take place, and the cycle begins again.

The water cycle happens in the stages of evaporation, condensation, precipitation, and collection. These stages involve water rising into the sky, forming clouds, falling to the ground, and then being collected into bodies of water. The water cycle never ends and constantly takes place.

# UNIT 05 How to Make Your Favorite Food

## Building Vocabulary p.36

| | |
|---|---|
| 1 stir | 2 crockpot |
| 3 undercook | 4 slice |

## Model Essay and Grammar in Writing p.38

### How to Make My Favorite Food

There are many foods I like, but my favorite food is pork chops with baked apples. It sounds complicated, but it is actually easy to make. There are only a few simple steps you need to follow.

(1)First, you need to prepare your ingredients. To make this meal, you need four pork chops, two apples, and some raisins. You must also have salt, brown sugar, cinnamon, cloves, and apple juice. In addition, you need a baking pan coated in oil, and you should heat the oven to 350 degrees Celsius.

(2)Next, peel the apples, slice them, and put them into the baking pan. (3)After that, put a handful of raisins on top of the apples. (4)Then, sprinkle some brown sugar, cinnamon, and cloves on the apples and raisins. (5)Now, put some salt on the pork chops and place them on the apples. (6)Then, put the pan into the oven and bake for around forty minutes.

(7)Last, you need to make the sauce. Pour some apple juice and brown sugar into a pan. Heat it to a boil and then simmer it for about ten minutes. When the pork chops are done, you can pour the sauce on them, or you can dip the pork chops or apples into the sauce.

Pork chops and apples is my favorite food, and it is not difficult to cook. Just prepare the ingredients, put the spices on the pork and apples, and cook everything in the oven. When the food is finished, you can enjoy a delicious meal.

# UNIT 06 Your Favorite Painting

## Building Vocabulary p.44

1 brushstrokes
2 creative
3 master painter
4 secondary colors

## Model Essay and Grammar in Writing p.46

### My Favorite Painting

The title of my favorite painting is *Son of Man*. It's (It is) a work of surrealism that was painted by René Magritte in 1964. The painting is totally awesome (impressive / beautiful / wonderful), and that is what makes it my favorite work of art.

The painting depicts a man standing in front of a stone wall. He's (He is) wearing a gray overcoat as well as a bowler hat, a white shirt, and a red tie. Behind the wall, there is a body of water that looks like a sea or ocean, and there's (there is) also a cloudy sky.

Those features are not what make the painting interesting though. What I find fascinating about it is that we cannot see the man's face clearly (the man's face can be seen clearly) because there is a green apple obscuring his face. The apple and some leaves are covering most of his face, so we cannot see who the man is (nobody can tell who the man is).

If you look closely, you will notice that you can see (A person who looks closely will be able to see) part of the man's eyes peeking out around the apple. In addition, the man's arm appears to be bending backward rather than forward. According to Magritte, *Son of Man* is a self-portrait. However, because the man's face cannot be seen, it might not really be Magritte. It could be anyone hiding behind the apple, and that's (that is) why I love this painting.

*Son of Man* by René Magritte is my favorite painting. I really wanna (want to) see this painting in real life because of how mysterious and intriguing it is.

# UNIT 07 The Rooms in Your Home

## Building Vocabulary p.50

1 appliances
2 dresser
3 basement
4 cramped

## Model Essay and Grammar in Writing p.52

### The Rooms in My Home

I live in a three-bedroom apartment with my family. Not only are there the three bedrooms, but my home contains a living room, a kitchen, and two bathrooms. Each room has its own special appearance and unique characteristics.

My bedroom is the smallest of the three bedrooms in my home. The major pieces of furniture in it are my bed, my desk, and my wardrobe. There is a large window overlooking a park, too. There are also a few posters of my favorite pop groups hanging on the walls.

The other two bedrooms belong to my parents and my older sister. While my parents' bedroom only has a bed and a wardrobe, my sister's bedroom has a desk like mine. Both of those bedrooms have pictures hanging from the walls as well.

As for the other rooms in my house, there is nothing special about the bathrooms. Each contains a sink, a toilet, and a shower. The kitchen also resembles a standard one in most people's homes. There are several appliances, including a stove, a microwave oven, a coffeemaker, and a refrigerator. The living room is comfortable and spacious. There is a large sofa big enough for everyone in my family, and there is a big-screen TV on the wall. Finally, there is a table where we eat our meals.

My home has lots of furniture and other items found in most people's homes. While there is nothing particularly special about my home, I think it looks great and love living there.

# UNIT 08 Your Characteristics

## Building Vocabulary p.56

1 responsible
2 describe
3 emotional
4 charming

## Model Essay and Grammar in Writing p.58

### My Characteristics

There are many words that could be used to describe my characteristics. However, if I had to choose just three, they would be friendly, hardworking, and curious.

I go out of my way to be friendly to others. I am also nice and considerate toward my friends, and I make an effort to become friends with people who look lonely. Last weekend, I saw a person at a café who looked a bit down. I went to his table and asked if I could sit with him. He agreed, and we started a conversation. By the time it ended, he looked much happier than before.

I am also a hardworking individual. It does not matter what kind of task, chore, or homework or work assignment I am doing. If I have something to do, I work hard to do it to the best of my ability. Thanks to this ability, I do good work and also complete it on time.

Finally, I consider myself a curious person. When I hear about something new, I get interested in it and try to learn more. <u>Two weeks ago, I was watching a TV program on ancient history. It was so interesting that I became curious about that period of time, so I went to the library to learn more about it.</u> That is just one example of how curious I can be.

Friendliness, the ability to work hard, and curiosity are three words that define me. They are some of my most important characteristics, and they have a big influence on my personality.

# 09 A Place You Would Like to Visit

**UNIT**

## Building Vocabulary p.62

| | |
|---|---|
| 1 itinerary | 2 cruise ship |
| 3 tropics | 4 safari |

## Model Essay and Grammar in Writing p.64

### Where I Would Like to Go in the Future

I would love to visit hundreds of places around the world. However, one place that <u>really</u> (Not necessary) stands out in my mind is Hawaii. If I could travel to Hawaii, it would be like a dream come true.

For starters, Hawaii has a tropical climate, so the weather is <u>pretty</u> (Not necessary) hot there all year long. In my home country, the weather is <u>very</u> (Not necessary) cold and snowy in winter. Last winter, there was snow on the ground for most of December and January. If I visited Hawaii in winter, I could forget about cold temperatures and <u>simply</u> (Necessary) enjoy my time there.

I am also a <u>very</u> (Not necessary) huge fan of the beach, and Hawaii has plenty of beautiful beaches. I love swimming and getting a suntan on the beach. I want to try snorkeling, <u>too</u> (Necessary). I heard it is possible to see numerous tropical fish close to shore by going snorkeling. That would be a great experience.

Lastly, Hawaii has some <u>totally</u> (Not necessary) interesting geology that I am interested in exploring. There are rainforests I want to trek through. Hiking to the top of Diamond Head, a mountain near Honolulu, and seeing the sun rise would be amazing.

I would also (Necessary) like to visit the volcanoes like Mauna Loa on one of the Hawaiian Islands. Visiting those places would literally (Not necessary) make my trip perfect.

Hawaii stands out as one place I would love to visit in the future. It has <u>really</u> (Not necessary) outstanding weather, great beaches, and unique geography. I hope to travel there one day.

# 10 Your Favorite Class

**UNIT**

## Building Vocabulary p.68

| | |
|---|---|
| 1 submit | 2 diploma |
| 3 discussion | 4 pass |

## Model Essay and Grammar in Writing p.70

### My Favorite Class

When I was a high school student, I was uninterested in learning. As a matter of fact, I was a poor student with terrible grades. <u>Then, I took Mr. Lambert's math class. At that moment, everything changed.</u> The class I took with him during my junior year of high school is my favorite class.

First of all, Mr. Lambert had a way of making the material he was teaching seem easy. I was never good at math, so I was not looking forward to his class. However, Mr. Lambert's explanations were so clear that I did well in his class. In fact, I rarely missed any problems and got A+'s on most of my tests.

Secondly, Mr. Lambert always encouraged the students to study hard and to do their best. <u>He believed all students could do math.</u> He stated this belief so much that everybody came to think it was true. <u>Many students performed well in his class.</u>

Third, Mr. Lambert did not just use class time to teach us math. <u>He taught us other things.</u> These included the importance of getting a good education, the need to work hard, and the need to believe in yourself. I gained a lot of confidence thanks to that class. <u>Today, I still remember it fondly.</u>

Mr. Lambert's math class is my favorite class of all time, and he helped me become a better student and person. To this day, I always visit him on Teacher's Day to give him a present and to thank him for helping me.

# UNIT 11 Recycling

## Building Vocabulary p.76

1 biodegradable
2 pollute
3 reuse
4 toxic

## Model Essay and Grammar in Writing p.78

### Everyone Should Recycle

I believe everyone should recycle. There are several positive results of recycling. In addition, if we do not recycle, there could be many negative effects. In my opinion, every person should recycle as much as possible.

First of all, recycling allows us to conserve our planet's natural resources. Many of the Earth's natural resources are nonrenewable ones, so there is a limited supply of them. For instance, metals, coal, oil, and gas are all nonrenewable resources. If we recycle materials that are made with them, then we can use fewer valuable resources and save them for future generations.

Another thing is that it is wasteful simply to throw away many items after using them. Landfills these days are full of plastic, glass, and metal products. Instead of throwing these items away, we should recycle them. These products can then either be reused or turned into other products that people can use.

Finally, if we do not recycle, there will be countless problems. For example, garbage dumps will become full of unrecycled products that do not break down for centuries. That will waste large amounts of land. In addition, many unrecycled items will be thrown onto the land and into the water and therefore create pollution. So not recycling would have the effect of harming the Earth.

Recycling can conserve natural resources and let us reuse them. It can also prevent the wasting of land and the creating of pollution. Because recycling has so many benefits, I think everyone should do it.

# UNIT 12 Voting

## Building Vocabulary p.82

1 rhetoric
2 candidates
3 represent
4 ballot

## Model Essay and Grammar in Writing p.84

### Lower the Voting Age

In my country, the voting age is eighteen, but that is too high. Instead, the voting age should be lowered to sixteen for a number of important reasons.

Sixteen-year-olds already act like adults in many ways, so we should treat them like adults by letting them vote. For instance, in my country, around thirty percent of sixteen-year-olds have jobs, which is adult behavior. They are taking part in the economy and paying taxes, so they should get to vote. Three of my teenage cousins have jobs. It is not fair that they cannot vote.

In addition, adults often complain that teenagers are not interested in politics or the political process. But only about sixty-five percent of eligible voters participated in the last election. Teens usually do not care about politics since they cannot vote, and that feeling extends to adulthood. But if teens were allowed to vote, many would get interested in politics. Then, the overall voter participation rate would increase.

Finally, we should not disregard the opinions of young people by preventing them from voting. A recent survey showed that seventy percent of teenagers hesitated to state their opinions because they felt that adults would ignore them. If the voting age were decreased, adults would have to listen to teens and their ideas.

It is imperative that the voting age be lowered to sixteen. Sixteen-year-olds work and pay taxes like adults. And voting will make them more interested in politics and obligate adults to listen to them and their opinions.

# UNIT 13 Pets

## Building Vocabulary p.88

1 adopt
2 veterinarian
3 treat
4 loyal

## Model Essay and Grammar in Writing p.90

### Dogs: The Best Pets

People keep numerous animals as pets, including dogs, cats, birds, fish, hamsters, and reptiles. Of all these animals, dogs are by far the best pets.

For one thing, dogs are incredibly loving animals. My family has a dog that is always happy to see us. When anyone in my family goes home, Rusty is at the door to greet us. Rusty also loves spending time with us and is a great pet. In contrast, we have a cat, too. Natasha spends time by herself and does not seem to care much about us.

In addition, you can do activities with dogs that you cannot do with other pets. Every day, I take Rusty out to the park to go for a walk. I throw a stick, and he fetches it. You cannot take a hamster, fish, or a snake out for a walk. Birds and cats do not fetch either. Those animals have fewer abilities than dogs do.

Yet another thing is that dogs have been known to save their owners' lives. I have read many stories about dogs that notify people assistance is needed when their owners suffer medical problems. Recently, there was a news story about a dog that rescued a baby from a fire. A pet cat would never do anything like that.

When it comes to pets, dogs are the best animals. They are loyal, you can do fun activities with them, and they just might save your life. Clearly, people should choose dogs when selecting new pets.

## UNIT 14 Chores

### Building Vocabulary p.94

1 chastise
2 garbage
3 babysit
4 burden

### Model Essay and Grammar in Writing p.96

#### Children Should Not Do Chores

When I was a child, my parents made me do chores. I felt like I was going to die (I did not enjoy doing them / I felt they were a burden) because they kept me from doing other activities. I therefore strongly oppose making children do chores.

For one thing, children need to enjoy their lives. When they are young, they ought to be outdoors playing with their friends or doing other fun activities. They do not need to be tortured (They do not need to be forced to clean their rooms) by having to clean their rooms, set the table, or do the laundry. They can do those chores later when they are teenagers.

For another thing, the children in my country are already busy because of school. When I was an elementary school student, I had tons of homework (I had a lot of homework). I also attended some private academies. I arrived home around eight at night, and then my parents had me do chores. I was so tired that I could barely move (I was exhausted), so that was unfair to me.

As a final note, children are too young to do chores well, so they will not do a satisfactory job. One of my chores was washing the dishes. I tried hard, but I was the worst dishwasher in the world (I was not good at washing the dishes). My mother was always disappointed, but there was nothing I could do. I was too young to be washing the dishes.

There is no reason to have children do chores. They need to have fun and are already busy because of school, and they will not do well anyway. For those reasons, parents should not make children do chores.

## UNIT 15 Video Games

### Building Vocabulary p.100

1 joystick
2 concentration
3 realistic
4 aim

### Model Essay and Grammar in Writing p.102

#### The Need to Play Video Games

I do not believe that video games are harmful. In fact, I believe that they provide a number of positive benefits, so I would encourage people to play video games as much as they can.

The first reason is an obvious one: Video games are highly entertaining. I play all kinds of games with my friends, but I especially like shooting games and role-playing games. I have gotten hundreds of hours of entertainment by playing some of these games. If you want something fun to do, video games are an inexpensive and safe activity to do.

The second reason is that video games can help you improve various skills. When I play shooting games, my hand-eye coordination improves. I have to notice all of the bad guys on the screen, aim the weapons, and shoot them. When I play with my friends, I learn about teamwork. By working as a team, we can do well and win the games.

The third reason is that when you play multiplayer online games, you can meet people from around the world. During these games, I sometimes talk to the other players. I have even become friends with some of them. These people live in countries around the world, so by playing video games, I have made some foreign friends.

I strongly urge everyone to play video games. They are fun and can help you improve various skills. And it is even possible to make friends while playing them.

## UNIT 16  A Story from Your Country's History

### Building Vocabulary  p.108

1  famous
3  funny

2  execute
4  tyrant

### Model Essay and Grammar in Writing  p.110

#### William Tell

My country is Switzerland, and William Tell is the most famous man from my nation. He is known as the Swiss national hero of liberty because thanks to him, Switzerland became free.

William Tell lived during the 1300s, when Switzerland was ruled by Duke Gessler, a tyrant. Gessler always demanded that people bow to him. But that was not enough. Once, he put his cap on a tall pole in a public square and insisted that people bow to it. Everyone did that except for one man: William Tell. He proudly walked past the pole.

Gessler became upset, so he had Tell and his son seized. Then, he ordered Tell's son to be put in the middle of the square, and an apple was placed on his head. He told Tell that if he could shoot the arrow off his son's head from 200 paces away, then he could go free.

Tell, an excellent archer, took out an arrow, aimed it, and let it fly. His son did not move an inch as the arrow struck the middle of the apple. As Tell ran to his son, another arrow fell from inside his coat. "Why do you have that second arrow?" asked Gessler. Tell responded, "If I had missed, this second arrow was meant for you." Not long afterward, Tell shot and killed Gessler with an arrow and in doing so, set his country free.

William Tell, one of the bravest men in my country's history, was a great man. Due to his actions, Switzerland became free and has remained that way for centuries.

## UNIT 17  A Scary Moment in Your Life

### Building Vocabulary  p.114

1  robbery
3  scared

2  drunk driving
4  crash

### Model Essay and Grammar in Writing  p.116

#### The Scariest Moment

I have not had very many scary moments in my life. However, there is one frightening event during a family trip that stands out in my mind.

Two years ago, my family went on a vacation to Australia, where we spent lots of time on the beach. One day, we decided to go snorkeling, so we bought tickets for a snorkeling trip and took a boat out to a coral reef in the ocean.

I was having a great time snorkeling and looking at all kinds of beautiful fish. Then, I heard some screaming. I put my head up out of the water and heard people shouting, "Get out of the water!" I looked around and saw some people on the boat pointing near me. I looked to where they were pointing and saw a huge fin above the water. It was a shark!

I could not believe my eyes. I immediately started swimming toward the boat. Everyone was yelling, "Hurry! Hurry!" I looked and saw that the fin was getting closer. By this time, I was the only person in the water. As I reached the boat, my father said, "Take my hand," and he reached down, grabbed my hand, and pulled me out of the water. Just then, an enormous shark swam right by the boat.

Having a close encounter with a shark was the scariest moment in my life. I could have been eaten by the shark, but thanks to my father and other people, I managed to survive.

## UNIT 18  A Time When You Helped Someone

### Building Vocabulary  p.120

1  devoted
3  lend

2  bankrupt
4  donation

### Model Essay and Grammar in Writing  p.122

#### Time When I Helped Someone

I like to help people whenever I have the opportunity to do so. A few years ago, I had the chance to assist my sister when she required some succor (help; assistance).

I had been saving my money because I wanted to purchase a new car. I almost had enough money, so I was starting to consider which kind of car I should procure (obtain, purchase) for myself. Then, my parents gave me some information about my sister. Apparently, she was thinking about dropping out of college because she could not afford the tuition anymore.

I called her up and talked to her about her problem. She informed me that her school had amplified (increased; raised) the price of tuition, so it was unaffordable for her. Even worse, she was just one semester away from graduation. Right there, I decided to give my sister the money she needed to afford school.

She was euphoric (extremely happy). She gladly accepted my offer and then went on to graduate from college. After that, she managed to find a great job that helped her get started on her career. A year later, she paid me back the lucre (money) even though I had told her that it was a gift. I felt great about being able to help my sister since it let her have a successful life.

Helping my sister when she needed the money stands out in my mind as a time when I helped someone. I was able to assist someone who needed help, and she truly appreciated it.

# UNIT 19 The Last Trip You Took

## Building Vocabulary p.126

1 cancelation
2 five-star hotel
3 translation
4 refreshed

## Model Essay and Grammar in Writing p.128

### My Last Trip

[Last summer, my family decided to take a trip because we had not gone anywhere together for a long time.] We thought about traveling abroad or going to the beach, but we decided to go camping instead.

There is a national park about two hours away from our home, so we packed our camping equipment, drove to the park, and went hiking in the woods. We found a nice place to pitch our tent near a lake and then started collecting wood to make a fire at night.

On the first day, we hiked in the forest and went fishing in the lake. We caught a few fish, so we planned to cook them for dinner. Fish roasted over an open fire tastes delicious. [When night came, we sat around the campfire, talked about our lives, and told some stories.]

The next three days were similar to the first one. We had a mostly relaxing time and became really close to one another on our trip. [Of course, camping in the woods was hard, and we got bitten by lots of bugs, but overall, we were all incredibly happy when it was time to pack up everything and drive back home.]

I had a great time on my last trip. Camping in the forest with my family for a few days was a wonderful experience. I hope that all of my trips in the future are as good as it was.

# UNIT 20 A Time You Learned a Valuable Lesson

## Building Vocabulary p.132

1 consideration
2 shopping spree
3 bravery
4 selfish

## Model Essay and Grammar in Writing p.134

### A Lesson I Learned

There have been several events in my life when I learned important lessons. One event (delete) happened when I was a middle school student. Because of that time in middle school (delete), I changed how I treated people.

Once, my class took a math test. Mathematics happened to be my best subject, so I did very well on the test (it / the exam). In fact, when the teacher returned the tests, I received a perfect score, but my best friend got an F because she had not studied. When I saw her grade, I started laughing, making her burst into tears.

A month later, my class took a history test. I did really poorly on the history test (it / the exam), but my best friend did not. However, when she saw how upset I was, she did not laugh at me. Instead, she comforted me and told me that it was all right and that I would do better the next time.

I immediately remembered how I had treated her. I felt awful about my treatment of her (that / how I had acted), so I immediately (delete) apologized. She graciously accepted my apology. From that incident, I learned the importance of being sympathetic to others. Rather than laughing at people when something bad happens, I needed to help them feel better.

Since then, I no longer make fun of people when they do poorly at something. Instead (On the other hand), I encourage them and help them gain confidence. That incident at school has remained in my memory for years, and it was definitely an important lesson I learned at school (delete).

# Appendix

# Punctuation Guide

## Terminal Points

1 Use a period (.) at the end of a declarative sentence.
I met my friend.

2 Use a question mark (?) at the end of an interrogative sentence.
Did you meet your friend?

3 Use an exclamation point at the end of an exclamatory sentence.
I met my friend!

NOTE: Do not overuse exclamation points. They should be extremely rare. Do not use multiple exclamation points either. There is no need to use !!!! at the end of a sentence. Finally, do not combine punctuation like ?! in your writing. Choose one form of punctuation and use only it.

## Pause Points

1 Use a semicolon (;) to connect two independent clauses.
I met my friend; however, he had to leave early.

2 Use a colon (:) to indicate that the information that follows either elaborates or summarizes on the information preceding it.
I met my friend: Mr. James Symington.

3 Use a comma (,) in the following situations:

in front of a coordinating conjunction joining two independent clauses
I met my friend, and we had a great time.

in a complex sentence that begins with a subordinating conjunction
Because I met my friend, we had a great time.

in a series combining three or more words, phrases, or sentences
I met my friends, my family members, and my coworkers.

in front of a relative pronoun
I met my friend, whom I have known for ten years.

to create an appositive
I met my friend, Andrea Smith, last night.

to write dates
I met my friend on January 21, 2019.

4 Use a dash (—) to indicate an interruption.
I met my friend—we have known each other for years—the other night.

## Quotes

Use double quotation marks (" ~ ") to indicate quoted speech.

1 Use a comma to separate the quoted part from the rest of the sentence.
"I met my friend," I said.

2 Use a period if the quotation comes at the end of the sentence.
I said. "I met my friend."

3 Use a question mark to ask a question in quoted speech. Put the question mark inside the quotation mark.
"Did you meet your friend?" she asked.

4 Put the question mark after the quotation mark if the quotation is not a question but the entire sentence is.
Do you think he said, "I met my friend"?

NOTE: British English often uses single quotes (' ~ '). In addition, the punctuation usually comes after the quotation marks.
'I met my friend', I said.

## Apostrophes

1 Use an apostrophe (') to show possession.
I met my friend's brother.

2 Use an apostrophe to create a contraction.
I didn't meet my friend.

## Hyphens

Use a hyphen (-) to create compound adjectives or nouns.
I met my next-door neighbor.

NOTE: If a noun follows a compound adjective, use a hyphen. If no noun follows a compound adjective, do not use a hyphen.
He is a serious-looking man.
The man is serious looking.

# Vocabulary Index

## UNIT 1

affect

efficient

future

improve

Internet of Things

neighborhood

recycle

renewable

sustainable

technology

transportation

## UNIT 2

diet

exercise

fitness

flexibility

health

muscles

nutrition

sports

stress

training

## UNIT 3

characteristic

friend

kindness

loyalty

optimism

relationship

successful

survey

tact

trustworthy

## UNIT 4

collection

condensation

ecosystem

erosion

evaporate

flood

precipitation

stage

storm

water cycle

## UNIT 5

bake

cook

favorite

food

heat

ingredient

meal

oven

roast

step

## UNIT 6

art gallery

color

depict

display

exhibit

fascinating

obscure

painting

self-portrait

work

## UNIT 7

apartment

appliance

bathroom

bedroom

furniture

garage

kitchen

living room

residence

yard

## UNIT 8

ability

characteristic

considerate

curious

define

extrovert

hardworking

introvert

prefer

quality

## UNIT 9

climate

dream

experience

itinerary

scenery

sightseeing

travel

trek

tour

visit

## UNIT 10

class
confidence
education
encourage
explanation
instructor
material
perform
style
teaching method

## UNIT 11

conserve
exhaust
landfill
nonrenewable resource
power
recycle
renewable resource
reuse
supply
waste

## UNIT 12

compulsory
disregard
election
eligible
lower
opinion
participate
political process
politics
vote

## UNIT 13

ability
activity
breed
fetch
keep
loyal
pet
save one's life
spend time with
take care of

## UNIT 14

assist
busy
chore
clean
have fun
laundry
oppose
private academy
unfair
vacuum

## UNIT 15

benefit
entertaining
game console
hand-eye coordination
improve
multiplayer online game
positive
release
video game
virtual reality

## UNIT 16

archer
arrow
brave
god
goddess
history
mythology
national hero
story
tyrant

## UNIT 17

alien
evil
fin
horror film
scary
scream
serial killer
shark
slasher film
snorkeling

## UNIT 18

animal shelter
appreciate
assistance
donation
help
litter
pay back
soup kitchen
tuition
volunteer

## UNIT 19

adventure

become close

campfire

camping

highlight

relaxing

safari

spend the night

travel abroad

trip

## UNIT 20

apology

burst into tears

cheat

comfort

laugh

lesson

life-changing

pass away

personal

valuable